# Book Reviews

"If you claim to be wrongfully accused or convicted of a crime, hope to God that Paul Ciolino agrees with you. An ancient warrior in a modern world, Ciolino has written an absorbing tale of justice gone wrong and his quest to right it."

—Patrick W. Picciarelli, author of *Mala Femina: A Woman's Life as the Daughter of a Don*

"Paul Ciolino is a tireless fighter against injustice. He views the subject of wrongful convictions with the perspective of an experienced insider."

—Eric Zorn, *Chicago Tribune* columnist

"As one of America's leading private investigators—the tough-talking, butt-kicking kind you thought existed only in the imaginations of Hollywood screenwriters—Paul Ciolino has spent decades helping to bring Chicago's guilty to justice and freeing her innocent from death row. When Ciolino talks about the criminal justice system, it pays to listen."

—James Rosen, White House correspondent, *FOX News*

"Politicians and prosecutors have become so tough on crime that they convict the innocent in a disturbing number of cases. That leaves the culprit free, the community unprotected, and an innocent person in prison. Fortunately for many of the wrongfully convicted, a private investigator, Paul Ciolino, has stepped forward—often working with volunteer lawyers and members of the media—to prove their innocence and show how the system failed."

—Stephen B. Bright, Executive Director for Southern Center on Human Rights

"Paul Ciolino gives us the benefit of decades of working as a private investigator digging up the truth. His wide-ranging books show his genuine passion for helping people during turbulent times. *In The Company of Giants* offers a masterfully original and practical perspective on how wrongful convictions happen, and what we can do about them."

—Elizabeth F. Loftus, Distinguished Professor of Psychology & Social Behavior, University of California at Irvine, Past President, American Psychological Society, Author of Eyewitness Testimony & Witness for the Defense.

"To successfully uncover the facts in cases of wrongful conviction requires years of experience, dogged determinism, and a detailed knowledge of criminal due process and investigation. Paul Ciolino embodies each of these qualities. He has dedicated his life to the pursuit of justice. His investigation skills are widely known and respected. This thoughtful and pragmatic book makes a significant contribution to field of wrongful conviction investigation. It will serve a needed purpose for university students, as well as seasoned practitioners."

—Robert Carl Schehr, Chair of the Department of Criminal Justice, Director of the Northern Arizona Justice Project, Northern Arizona University.

"Paul Ciolino is a renowned and sometimes reviled investigator who exposes the underbelly of the system's disgraceful treatment of the wrongfully convicted criminal defendant. *In the Company of Giants* is mandatory reading for every investigator who has an interest in justice and wants to do something about it. This is a stark examination that shows you how to fix the wrongful conviction case."

—Julius Buddy Bombet, Former President of Louisiana State Board of Private Investigators

"Paul Ciolino is not the private investigator that you see in a million series on television. He is the real deal and a lot more. Beneath a brilliant tough exterior is a tremendous heart, a feeling for people that he has the courage to help no matter how difficult or even dangerous the situations are. Having created Kojak, he is the real Kojak and more."

—Abby Mann, Oscar & Emmy Award winning author of *Judgment at Nuremberg, Indictment, The McMartin Trial, Kojak* television series, & the made for television movie on Dr. Martin Luther King

"Some of his critics have called investigator Paul Ciolino's street tactics "like a bull in a china shop." Those of us who have worked with him and respect his skill as a private investigator will tell you that there was a real killer hiding in that china shop and Paul found him. When innocent people are facing the executioner's axe, we need people like Paul who are willing to challenge a system gone haywire. His friends have been encouraging him for years to share his insights for righting the wrongs we all see too often. Thanks, Paul."

—Don C. Johnson, CLI, Past President, Indiana Society of Professional Investigators and Editor, *PI Magazine, the Journal of Professional Investigators.*

"For those who care about justice, and especially those who want to do something about injustice, Paul Ciolino's *In the Company of Giants* is must reading. Defense lawyers, judges, prosecutors, private investigators, journalists, and students aspiring to careers in those fields will find the book at once instructive on a practical level and engrossing as a literary product."

—Rob Warden, Executive Director, Center on Wrongful Convictions, Northwestern University School of Law

"Paul Ciolino is one of the nation's leaders in obtaining freedom for people who have been falsely convicted of murder—convictions which leave the actual, and dangerous, perpetrators on the street. This book explains his techniques for investigations."

—Lawrence R. Velvel, Dean, Massachusetts School of Law

"Time and time again Paul Ciolino has used his brain, moxie and heart to free the innocent. His success in criminal defense work is unparalled in the profession due to his unique combination of book and street smarts. Read and learn from one of the best in the business who always tells it like it is."

—Steven L. Kirby, President, Edward R. Kirby & Associates, CII, CFE

"*In the Company of Giants* details a no-nonsense approach to criminal investigations that focuses on real consequences. A street-savvy, skillful investigator, Paul Ciolino is committed to righting wrongs, providing the reader with practical information about how the justice system works, and sometimes fails."

—Eileen Halpin, Associate Director, The Criminal Justice Clinic, The John Marshall Law School

"Most private investigators get into this profession for the bucks but every once in a while, a man emerges from the profession that is fighting for a cause. When it comes to the wrongfully accused, that man is Paul Ciolino. This man is hard-nosed, street smart, controversial and VERY effective."

—Ralph Thomas, author *How To Find Anyone Anywhere, Professional's Guide To Physical Surveillance, The Countermeasures Cookbook, How To Investigate By Computer, Piracy Investigations for Private Investigators* and *Master Guide To Online Searching*

"I am the living example of why this book is so important. I was wrongfully convicted and I spent 16 years on Illinois Death Row for seven homicides I didn't commit. When I was released and pardoned in 2003 it was because of the tactics and strategies described herein. In the Company of Giants will hopefully save you or a loved one from a similar fate."

—Madison Hobly, Chicago, Illinois

# In The Company of Giants

# In The Company of Giants

◆

## The Ultimate Investigation Guide for Legal Professionals, Activists, Journalists & the Wrongfully Convicted

*Paul J. Ciolino*

To George,
One of my Hero's!
Best wishes

*Paul Ciolino*

iUniverse, Inc.
New York  Lincoln  Shanghai

# In The Company of Giants
## The Ultimate Investigation Guide for Legal Professionals, Activists, Journalists & the Wrongfully Convicted

iUniverse books may be ordered through booksellers or by contacting:

iUniverse
2021 Pine Lake Road, Suite 100
Lincoln, NE 68512
www.iuniverse.com
1-800-Authors (1-800-288-4677)

ISBN-13: 978-0-595-34813-8 (pbk)
ISBN-13: 978-0-595-67159-5 (cloth)
ISBN-13: 978-0-595-79542-0 (ebk)
ISBN-10: 0-595-34813-0 (pbk)
ISBN-10: 0-595-67159-4 (cloth)
ISBN-10: 0-595-79542-0 (ebk)

Printed in the United States of America

The most pleasurable part of writing a book is this, the dedication. If you're honest, you'll admit that sometimes you give this part more thought then you do the content of the book. I don't think that I did this in this case, but I do this with great pleasure and respect to those who this book is dedicated.

Only the people who I tortured, harassed and generally became a big pain in the ass to throughout the pregnancy and delivery of this book will read this part. I felt I owed it to all of you to acknowledge your good nature and overall brilliance. I say that because your great qualities are all reflected in this book. The other people who will read this section are the law enforcement personnel whom I so frequently reference during this book. In addition to not having a sense of humor when they are being singled out, they have a tendency to have long memories. In that spirit, I figured that my friends might as well enjoy some of their future wrath.

I have been blessed with remarkable support, love and friendship throughout the years from many different sources. Personally, I have been gifted with the love and support of Elizabeth Reed, my fiancé and best friend. A great trial attorney in her own right, she always acts with dignity, class, and intelligence. She is the rock that holds our family together. Her moral compass keeps us all pointed in the true direction.

Garrett Ordower who graciously edited this mess. Your patience is incredible.

Additionally, there are a number of people who have by their actions have continually motivated me to be the best that I can be: Rob Warden and David Protess of Northwestern University, they showed all of us the way. Their contribution to this whole wrongful conviction buisness is immeasurable. They will never receive the credit that they are due.

Andrea Lyon, director of The Center for Justice in Capital Cases at DePaul University Law School in Chicago. A true friend and a warrior who has fought the fight for more years then most of us have been around.

Kenny Adams who, without question, is one of the bravest, most moral, and finest human beings **to** ever come down the pike. In Chapter One I chronicle Kenny's struggle and fight for freedom. I'm afraid I did not do him justice. That's impossible because people like Kenny Adams are the reason that we all continue to fight this fight.

Steve Bright, the director of The Southern Center for Human Rights in Atlanta. A great friend and supporter who has always been in the trenches, and has never thought about leaving them. If anybody ever deserved to be a United States Supreme Court Justice, it's Steve Bright. His humanity, genius, and intelligence humble all of us.

Bruce Ellison, my dear friend and colleague and perhaps one of the greatest trial attorneys in America today. Bruce has defended the Native Americans in South Dakota since Wounded Knee. His understanding and defense of our first citizens in the face of American's continuing disgraceful treatment of them is without equal.

Sheila Murphy retired Cook County judge from Chicago. Judge Murphy has always followed the law and enforced it with compassion and common sense. She has been responsible for saving dozens of individuals form wrongful convictions. She has, and will always be, one of those people whose life has impacted thousands.

Former Illinois Governor George H. Ryan is unquestionably the bravest politician to ever serve in Illinois. Against all political advice and self-preservation tendencies that most politicians have finely tuned, Governor Ryan did the right thing. He listened to his conscience and saved countless lives. He stepped forward when no one in his position had ever done so before. His act of bravery in the face of total opposition will remain one of the shining examples of *selflessness* in this century.

Dennis Culloton was the former press secretary to Governor Ryan. Dennis' title will never reveal just how much of an impact he had on the whole commutation effort in Illinois. Dennis is an individual who is true to his word and heart.

Journalists Doug Longuini, CBS News, John Mondello, CBS News, Dave Savini, CBS News Chicago, Bryan Smith, Chicago Magazine, Susan Zirinsky, CBS News, Maurice Tamman, Atlanta Journal-Constitution, and Jim Avila, ABC News. It is because of people like you, that justice is eventually served and lost lives are reclaimed. A special thanks to the late Paul Hogan of NBC News Chicago. You showed the way.

To all of my friends who troll in the federal, state, and county public defender offices in America. To the attorneys, investigators, law clerks and paralegals who really do conduct "God's Work" for the true sake of justice.

To Rob Mitchell, who simply restored my faith and has been a true friend. He is a man that walks the walk and never waivers in his beliefs.

Special thanks to attorneys Fred Whitehurst & Craig Cooley, who so graciously shared their expertise and writings on DNA & laboratory misconduct.

Finally, to my fellow investigators from all over the world who have taught me much and continue to advise and assist with dignity, honor, and class.

To all of you, you have my never ending respect & love.

*Paul Ciolino, February 2005, Chicago.*

# *Contents*

# Foreword By:

✦

*Dennis Culloton, former press secretary to*
*Illinois Governor George H. Ryan*
*January 2005*

Where I grew up, on the Northwest Side of Chicago, where cops and firefighters and thick-forearmed Streets and Sanitation workers lived, you often judged a guy by whether or not you'd want him watching your back.

Paul Ciolino, first and foremost, is the type of guy who has got your back.

Then we'd judge a guy's toughness with the dark alley test: whether you'd want to run into him in a dark alley. Having seen him operate up close, I can tell you, if Paul Ciolino was looking for you, and you were between him and justice for his client, the answer is an emphatic no. He'd take you down or die trying.

When I first met Paul, I was a young reporter in the late 1980s covering a trial of a suburban woman who ran a day care center. She stood accused of unspeakable crimes against the children in her care. The news coverage leading up to the trial was breathless and dramatic. Reporters painted a picture of a monstrous woman who abused children—"every parent's nightmare." The coverage was based largely on the information provided to reporters by police and Cook County prosecutors. It was dramatic and heart breaking. The stories sold papers and grabbed ratings. They were also, as it turned out, untrue, according to a jury of 12 men and women. I won't drag her name through the mud once again.

The defense counsel was up against one of the Cook County State's Attorney's top prosecutors and, as will happen in "heater cases," the entire Cook County treasury. He was competent in his defense of this woman, an attractive and demure mother, grandmother and wife with a loving family surrounding her. But the case was his to lose. In my mind, the acquittal was won before the trial started, by the work of a hard-nose private eye, straight out of the casting room for the next Philip Marlowe send-up.

In this book, you'll hear about how Paul Ciolino, private eye, took some journalism students out of the classroom and into real world Crime Reporting 101, to help them unravel now infamous wrongful convictions cases. On a shoestring budget, Paul along with a couple of other veteran investigators and journalists—including a couple of dedicated, passionate investigative reporters, Northwestern's Dave Protess and Rob Warden—worked together to prove the innocence the so-called "Ford Heights Four." It was a scandalous wrongful conviction for a double murder of four innocent men. The case was a house of cards, based in large part on the testimony of a mentally challenged teen-aged girl, Paula Gray, who, implicated the innocent men after police, literally and figuratively, put a gun to her head in a withering two-day interrogation. As you'll hear, a judge named Sheila Murphy put an end to the nightmare.

Helping to exonerate the Ford Heights Four should have been a high point of his career, a once-in-a-lifetime achievement.

That should have been the impetus for change. But in Chicago, injustice was just another day at the office. It took lies, videotape and the wrongful conviction of Anthony Porter to do what the 10 wrongful convictions that came before him could not do—halt the deeply flawed Illinois death penalty system.

To anyone who has met him, Anthony Porter comes across as a man who has lived a hard life with a limited IQ. Despite that he carries with him an infectious optimism that, even after nearly 17 years of sensory deprivation in a stark cell on death row, he managed to maintain. At worst he's the type of guy who might be a nuisance to local police. But Chicago Police and Cook County prosecutors said he was guilty of a 1982 double murder in a Chicago park. They had a witness. They won a conviction and secured a death sentence.

Forty-eight hours from death, Anthony Porter had ordered his last meal and been measured for his burial suit. But Professor Larry Marshall and the Northwestern Center on Wrongful Convictions won a delay so that the court could evaluate whether he was mentally competent to be killed by the state. That gave Protess and his Northwestern University Medill journalism students the chance to work once again with Ciolino. This was his finest hour. It started with a look at the crime scene. You'd need X-ray vision to say what the main eyewitness purported to see. The "eyeball," as eyewitnesses are called at the infamous Cook County courthouse at 26th and California, recanted his testimony to Paul and the students. The case of the People v. Anthony Porter quickly started to unravel.

It ended with Ciolino visiting Alstory Simon at his humble abode in Milwaukee. Armed with video camera, Ciolino had a message. He was going to come away from his visit with Alstory Simon telling the truth.

Soon, Anthony Porter, who went to prison before cell phones, cable and VHS in Reagan's first term, was running out from behind bars a free man for the first time in 17 years, making a joyous leap into the arms of Protess before the eyes of the national media. Once again the exoneration was won by plain old detective work.

Porter's case gave a shot in the arm to a team of reporters at the Chicago Tribune who documented the shameful condition of the Illinois capital punishment system. We were sending men to die based on the testimony of jailhouse snitches, with defendants represented by disbarred or suspended lawyers trying cases before biased juries with unreliable eyeball witnesses. Check out the reporting of Steve Mills, Maury Poseley and Ken Armstrong.

It was those indisputable facts and the haunting vision of Anthony Porter that convinced an Illinois governor, George H. Ryan, to halt executions in Illinois. A pharmacist by training, Governor Ryan couldn't understand how a system of laws could be so flawed.

I served as his press secretary and was, along with colleagues like Deputy Governor Matt Bettenhausen, subjected countless times to the Governor's frustration with the system he once believed in on blind faith. "How does this happen?" he bellowed to us time and again.

The bigger question is what would have happened, had not a hard-nosed, smart-aleck, street-smart investigator named Paul Ciolino, with journalism students in tow, not uncovered the truth? The answer is—with no evidence exonerating Anthony Porter, no light being shed on the other flawed death penalty cases—more than one innocent man might have been killed by the state.

I saw his fierce dedication to justice firsthand. Ciolino worked to beat the clock to bring every shred of evidence to the attention of the Governor as he weighed his historic January 2003 decision to commute the sentences of 167 death row inmates and pardon four of the men. "They can't get relief," he said as he slapped reams of files on the wrongfully convicted on coffee table in an office at Chicago's St. Mary's church.

Should they live or should they die? It is a decision I have come to believe no man should make. But as long as there is an ultimate punishment, there will be a need for investigators of ultimate dedication. Here's all you need: a fierce sense of justice; an expansive sense of humor; the ability to endure long hours; disappointment and, at times, very little pay; and the look of a guy you wouldn't want to meet in a Chicago alley. Faint of heart need not apply.

Many have questioned the motivations of George H. Ryan since January 2003. Most of my job as press secretary was consumed with answering the constant barrage of charges of corruption in his former office. He has since been indicted and as of this writing is awaiting trial. The growing movement of people concerned with the fairness or morality of our capital punishment system found they had an unlikely ally in the 40-year politician and pharmacist from Kankakee, a lifelong Republican who, when presented with the facts, decided to follow his conscience rather than political dogma. I know it took a great deal of courage to make a principled stand and halt the machinery of death in Illinois.

But it took a great deal more to uncover the truth beneath the layers and layers of muck, deceit and incompetence in the state's capital punishment system. If there was no Ciolino, the truth might never be known. He might not win a popularity vote. Lord knows he won't win a beauty contest. But he can sleep at night.

Even the most bleeding heart liberal civil rights lawyer will tell you everyone in prison says they are innocent but most are not. They've committed crimes beyond most of our imaginations. But in Illinois, we have a dubious achievement. We've documented that more of our inmates are innocent than any of us cares to admit. It goes against our very American belief system.

But with so many other things to worry about, especially in the post September 11th world, our society spends little time being concerned with the wrongfully incarcerated.

If you want to be one of the few and the proud who fight for them get used to this: no one wants to listen to you; no one wants to see you win; and everyone, perhaps even the inmate, will hate you. If you are doing your job right, you'll find that often times so did the system—that the right criminal was convicted and sentenced fairly and justly. But here's hoping you'll find the cases where the system didn't work. No pressure, but someone's life might depend on it.

So you want to fight for the wrongfully convicted? Read on and see if you have what it takes.

Dennis Culloton
February, 2005.

# Preface to This Edition

The author would like to thank all of his enemies (real & imagined) for purchasing and reading selected sections of this soon-to-be bestseller. First and foremost, the purchasing of this fine tome allows me to continue my numerous and lifelong bad habits. For example, I love to drink, gamble, and spend outrageous amounts of money on high-performance sports cars. I love antiques, exotic travel, and most of all, having the time to write stuff that makes me look like a world authority on any number of subjects.

I would like to thank the renegade cops and prosecutors who lie, cheat, and manufacture evidence. This creates general havoc in a justice system that is already overburdened with enough nonsense to keep myself and my colleagues gainfully employed for at least three or four more generations. I would like to acknowledge right-wing, and occasionally left-wing, moronic TV personalities who don't know shit from granola about criminal defense functions and issues. Without your able assistance, I would be out chasing errant husbands and wives. You give me reason to live some days.

Now in the spirit of interpretive glasnost, I would like to save you the reader some time and trouble. Skip this part, the dedication and index. Skip chapters 7 & 8. I wrote them and even I barely understand them. They weren't fun to write. I only wrote them so I would have a small degree of credibility. Skip the words with more then three syllables. Skip the reviews. I bribed and terrorized my friends to write them.

The author would also like to acknowledge his propensity to exaggerate and his tendency to BS a little, so that he looks good or bad, or even worse, yet both, so that I can come off a lot nicer then I really am. I would also like to acknowledge that no, I am not the only person to ever do this, but I am the only one that has a current book contract to do so.

I would like to seriously tip my hat to the Men & Women of The United States Armed Forces. I hope and pray that you all come home whenever you feel like it.

I hope that you get to fly at least business class (free). I hope that you come home to a grateful and appreciative citizenry. If we aren't appropriately grateful, feel free to hang a boot in the nearest offender's ass. This is the least we can offer after you have all performed in magnificent ways that showed us all just how much honor and bravery you posses collectively and individually. I am especially grateful to the Marines of the 2$^{nd}$ Battalion, Task Force 24, known as "The Mad Ghosts," specifically Sgt. Thomas W. Wasiel & Major Sean M. Sullivan of Chicago.

I would like to mention that I love the White Sox and anybody who beats the Cubs. I love the implicit logic of instant replay, a well-made martini, and Labrador Retrievers.

I would also like to recommend to the folks who issue law licenses in the United States that they reduce law school from three years to two for criminal defense lawyers. Instead of the third year of torts, real estate law, and other snooze subjects, they can spend that third year in a maximum security prison.

Yes, any attorney who is going to practice criminal law (especially prosecutors) should have to spend a year in the local gulag with Bubba and his friends. They would then be a little more careful about the Constitution, Bill of Rights, and other bothersome documents and principles.

Finally, many thanks again to all of my mentors who have saved me from myself on more then one occasion. I hope that you see a little bit of yourself in these pages.

# The Wrongful Conviction Case

✦

## VERITAS VALET VITAE
## ("The Truth Is Worth One's Life.")

Most investigative books are titled, *How to do that* and *How to do this*, and *How to make a million dollars sitting on your ass while playing solitaire on your computer.* I thought about the title of this book before I put one word down. Some of the titles were typical, some were boring, but most of them were unprintable.

I chose *In the Company of Giants* because that is where I most often find myself. The people who have mentored me, the men and woman who I have worked with, they are Giants in both their character and action. If I have been given one absolute blessing in life, and if there is one thing that I will miss after I'm gone from this world, it will be my colleagues who have shared and bled selflessly for this struggle in fairness and equity.

The heart, the pain and suffering of Kenny Adams, the brilliance of Andrea Lyon, the intellectual genius of Steve Bright, these are the secrets of this quest for justice. The logic and common sense of David Protess and Rob Warden, the personal and professional sacrifice of former Illinois Governor George Ryan, these are the things of which memories are made.

The spirit and selfless acts of courage displayed by former Chief Judge Sheila Murphy, attorneys Jack Rimland, Bruce Ellison, Elizabeth Reed, this is what motivates and drives me to the best I can. The backbreaking work of my investigative colleagues, who humble me with their efforts, are unforgettable and remarkable in both word and deed.

The creativity and brilliance of journalists Doug Longuini, John Mondello, Dave Savini, Steve Mills, Maury Possley, and others in their industry is the literal straw that has stirred the drink. Their work brings to the American public's living rooms the unfairness of it all. It displays in living color what those of us in the trenches already know: That the system is broken, it isn't fair, and it is often out of control in the name of patriotism and law and order.

*In The Company of Giants* is not going to solve all of your problems in a wrongful conviction case. It is not filled with lists and explicit "how to" suggestions. Its purpose is simple:

Find something that you can use, that will motivate you to work harder, something that will help you turn the corner in your case. This book, like the wrongful conviction investigation itself, is not about checklists. It is not that simple. Personally, I value all of those things and they have their place, but not here. This book is meant to give you an edge, an idea, a thought as to how you are going to get over the hump in any given situation.

In America, our Constitution and the Bill of Rights, in theory at least, guarantee each of us a fair trial should we be charged with a criminal offense. They guarantee that we are innocent until proven guilty. They guarantee an appeal process. They guarantee a trial by a jury of our peers. I believe in this with all my being. However, the fact is that these guarantees really guarantee nothing. It is my humble opinion that you will only obtain these rights if you have a competent team of professionals fighting for you in an effort to ensure that these guarantees are administered fairly and equally. If you don't, say goodbye, because you are on your way to your own special version of hell.

A well-funded government that is geared towards revenge and punishment is what we are up against. Clearly, in every case in which we find ourselves, there sits across the aisle in the courthouse a team of prosecutors who believe that we are the reincarnation of evil. Otherwise, if we weren't, they reason, why would we be defending this despicable human being? This is where the battle begins.

I have given this much thought throughout the years. The prosecutors and police are very much like us: hardworking, diligent, and interested in justice. The common denominators are numerous. So what's the problem? Well, I think the problem is a very basic one. As human beings, and especially as Americans, we are all pretty much cut from the same cloth. We are all interested in justice, at least in its most basic premise.

C.S. Lewis, arguably the most influential Christian writer of the last 100 years speaks to this very issue in his book *Mere Christianity*. He writes about the moral struggle and impulses that people experience. Lewis talks about the fact that the most dangerous thing a person can do is to take a good moral impulse and set it up as something you must do at any cost. When you do that, you leave out the good impulse of justice. When you leave out justice because of your other moral impulses, all kinds of bad stuff starts happening. For instance, faking evidence in trials, promoting and/or allowing false testimony, and so forth.

Herein lies the root of the issue: Justice, morality, and freedom. This is what our fight is about. This is what it boils down to for me, and I hope for you as well. Money is nice. Professional recognition by our peers is great. Warm and fuzzy media stories about our quest for justice are ego-enriching. But, at the end of the day, it is about our most basic and dearest God-inspired Constitutional rights as Americans. This is what the wrongful conviction case is about, and this is why we find ourselves doing this work.

When I started in this buisness in 1981, I didn't know what a criminal defense case was. I was naïve, ignorant, and clueless. Some 24-years later, I'm well-informed, but still fairly perplexed as to why these cases keep happening.

I've learned a lot about human nature, politics, and why these cases occur. I've learned to see the danger signs early. I can spot a wrongful conviction case pretty damn fast. But, for the life of me, I cannot understand why these cases are happening. As fast as we correct one wrong, another five have taken place.

The good news is that we in the criminal defense community have job security forever. The bad news is, of course, we will never lack worthy causes. The government and the politicians will see to that. I should mention that I mostly speak to the legal professional here, as that is the group that generally does all the heavy lifting in these cases. If you are sitting in a jail cell and reading this, make no mistake, you are our main concern.

If you are the client, defendant, inmate, whatever you are currently called, your ultimate freedom is our goal. You are why we do what we do. Your freedom is of the utmost importance and the highest priority to the professionals. The illegal and immoral taking of your freedom is, as far as I am concerned, the worst possible wrong that a free society can commit against one of its citizens.

There have been occasions where I have received too much credit for my work in these cases. There have also been occasions where not only did I not receive the credit I deserved, but those who had limited involvement would actually lie about their level of participation in a given case. I guess that I would summarize my participation as necessary and sometimes critical, but let there be no mistake, overturning one of these nightmares has always been a team effort.

I have taken a lot of shots at lawyers and other professionals in this book. They generally deserve it. After the police and prosecutors who start these nightmares, the people that we work with are the next biggest problem. Let me state right now that investigators share the blame equally, including me.

The point is that we all make mistakes. We all have a bad day, get too busy with other matters, and have mental lapses when we shouldn't. Most importantly, all of us have had wives, husbands, partners that have just wreaked havoc in our lives. (When a client who is locked up starts bitching about the fact that he is locked up, I always respond, "Try being married for twenty years, that's torture.")

That is why this is always a team effort. It is a team effort because when one member of the team falls down someone will pick him or her up. Ego, academic credentials, and titles have to be put aside. If the team does not function as one, the client suffers.

I am hopeful that in this book you will be able to steal one idea that will help you overturn a wrongful conviction. That is all it takes, a lot of determination and one good idea. My goal with this book is to give you some hope against the impossible. Overturning a wrongful conviction is, in sports parlance, akin to winning the World Series in the bottom of the ninth with two outs, the bases loaded, and down by three. You launch one into the bleachers. That is about how often you will win one of these.

Youth, naiveté, and positive thinking can only take you so far. Extreme hard work, dedication, and attention to detail always carry the day.

If you think that you are going to solve the mysteries of life from your office chair, put the book down, send it back and I'll refund your money.

There are no easy remedies here. Every successful wrongful conviction case that I have been involved with has generally taken years to overcome. When it hasn't, (Anthony Porter took about three months), the stars and the moon aligned perfectly and we struck gold.

Patience and wisdom win out. Short cuts and whimsical actions will destroy your case. Hopefully, we as a group have learned something about these cases. Generally we are wiser and worldlier then we were 10 or 20 years ago. If you haven't paid attention, you might be in deep water.

The prosecutors have taken some beatings and they have learned from those experiences. They have formulated a general plan that frustrates, delays, and conceals their true motivation. Simply put, they have learned from their mistakes and gotten a whole lot smarter then they were years ago.

Our job gets harder by the day. We have enjoyed many victories. We have climbed many mountains, but the basic fight continues. We are the true supporters of the Constitution and the people's rights. We are what generally stands between alleged justice and politics. We all too often find ourselves alone on that island with no help in sight. We only have each other and we should always be mindful of that fact.

Wrongful convictions have been around as long as the justice system has been operating in the United States. The reasons that people are falsely accused and wrongfully convicted are numerous. The solution to righting these wrongs is gut-wrenching and painful for the wrongfully convicted and their families. This book is meant to be a guide through those treacherous waters.

The author has been involved in dozens of these cases throughout the United States, Canada and Great Britain. Throughout the years he and his staff have pretty much seen it all. They have fortunately enjoyed many more successes then failures. The purpose of this book is to assist the investigator, attorney, family member, activist, or journalist in their quest for true justice.

Throughout the last 20-plus years, several patterns of significant behavior have become evident in almost every wrongful conviction case they have undertaken. In addition to helping you navigate through the minefield of tragedy in a wrongful conviction case, this book should also assist you in the investigation of a case that has not yet turned into a wrongful conviction, but is at the pretrial stage.

In the last several years, there has been a virtual explosion of "Innocence Projects" throughout the United States. With the best of intentions, well-meaning and honorable people started these projects. Ten years ago they were nonexistent. However, today we have them in almost every state. Unfortunately, this does not translate into instant success for the hundreds of wrongfully convicted. Quite the contrary. This often brings false hope to those who are rotting in prison for crimes they did not commit.

Let there be no mistake, money and funding play a huge part. It isn't that justice is for sale, which is a popular misconception. I have worked with well-funded clients, and of course with people who have zero funds. The well-funded and bank-rolled client enjoys more of an equal footing with the government and its unlimited resources. All things being equal, we will generally whip anyone, if we have the same resources. Money does help as long as it is used wisely. Money gains us otherwise denied access to the courthouse. Overcoming a lack of funding is not impossible, as long as we remain creative and fluid.

I hope this book will help bring some order to the chaos that we so frequently encounter when presented with a potential wrongful conviction. The single biggest problem that we encounter with a new case is the lack of organization and a plan for attacking it. We often spend more time "straightening" out the file than working on it. We are almost always presented with a train wreck as opposed to a well-organized and cohesive document. This is problematic in the respect that we often spend weeks or months attempting to figure out the basics. Hopefully we will be able to provide you some insight that will save us all a lot of trouble.

Throughout this text you will be constantly reminded and told about specific instances of police and prosecutorial misconduct. Frankly, this aspect of wrongful convictions is all too often the single biggest reason for a wrongful conviction and thus we pay a lot of attention to this issue. Having said that, we would be remiss if we did not mention that for every corrupt, lazy, incompetent and overzealous investigator or prosecutor there are literally thousands of them who do attempt to do the right thing.

As with sensational crimes and even more sensational criminals, there is an over-abundance of attention paid to them. Just as true is the fact that the bad cops and the bad prosecutors take away from the honest and hardworking people in the criminal justice system. We are not anti-law enforcement, we are pro-justice. Sometimes we are accused of being the former, but the simple fact is that we only report what is factual and provable in a court of law. The damage is done long before we ever become involved.

Finally, I am hopeful that if you take nothing else from this book, you take some heart. Because, that is what will get you over the hump in these cases. It will not be legal brilliance or technical proficiency—it will be heart. It will not be your fantastic investigative intuition—it will be your heart.

In every successful outcome I've been involved with, it has been somebody's character and heart that has saved the day. It has been an individual—be it investigator, journalist, attorney or family member—with the extra degree of motivation that has carried the day. It is almost never one single act, but rather a number of acts that have done the job.

In closing, I would like to share a prayer that my colleague Steve Bright read to Yale Law School graduates at their May 1999 commencement. I thought that this prayer was very appropriate for what we do on a daily basis.

> Lord, open my eyes that I may see the needs of others; open my ears that I may hear their cries; open my heart so that they need not be without succor; let me not be afraid to defend the weak because of the anger of the strong, nor afraid to defend the poor because of the anger of the rich.

> Show me where love and hope and faith are needed, and use me to bring them to those places.

> And so open my eyes and my ears that I may this coming day be able to do some work of peace for thee. Amen.

So, if you think that this book is the answer to a wrongfully convicted individual's freedom, you are mistaken. In the end it will be your heart, your tenacity and your willingness to do anything or go anywhere to succeed.

If I were able to motivate you to do that, I have done my job. It is up to you to do the rest.

# 1

## Kenny Adams A Primer on Wrongful Convictions & Heart

*"I have a dream that my four little children will one day live in a nation where they will not be judged by the color of their skin, but the content of their character."*

—Martin Luther King, Summer 1963

**State's Attorney:** *"Kenny, all you have to tell us is that you and your codefendants did the murder and you can go home the day you testify."*
**Kenny Adams:** *"Is that car from the department of corrections that brought me here still out there?"*
**State's Attorney:** *"Yeah, why?"*
**Kenny Adams:** *"Well, take me and put my ass right back in it because I know I didn't kill those people and they (Adams' three codefendants) didn't do it either."*

You might think the above statement is a pretty easy thing to say if you are an innocent and an honorable person. Well, think again, because when Kenny Adams made that statement, he had already been rotting in Menard Correctional Center for almost 18 years. And it wasn't the first, the second or even the third time he had turned down the Cook County State's Attorney's seemingly generous offer. Kenny had been incarcerated in a prison that has a reputation for breaking down the most hardened criminals from Chicago's gang-infested streets. Mass murderers, powerful and ruthless gang leaders, sexual predators and the worst of the worst call Menard home.

Menard is not "Club Fed" where the inmates spend their days playing cards and figuring out how to prepare a bootleg meal of steak and pasta. No, Menard is and was the hellhole of the Illinois prison system. Located in Southern Illinois amongst the rolling soybeans and cornfields, Menard is an institution that would

1

make Saddam Hussein blush. At Menard you are told by both the guards and inmates, "We'll have you screaming like a little bitch in 24 hours. In six months we'll have you wearing a dress and lipstick." Kenny neither screamed nor wore lipstick.

At Menard, the inmates really do run the asylum. Unfortunately for Kenny he was neither a gang member nor a criminal. Menard was not by any stretch of the imagination an easy place to do time, especially for Kenny Adams.

Kenny was raised in East Chicago Heights (later renamed Ford Heights), about one hour south of Chicago, near the Indiana border. He was the fifth-oldest of fifteen children, raised by his mother, Claudette, and stepfather, Joe Hurley.

Unlike many of the kids in his neighborhood, Kenny never received so much as a parking ticket from the police. An excellent baseball player and a good student, Kenny was the kind of kid that everybody loved.

Unfortunately, the Cook County Sheriff's Police investigators and the Cook County prosecutors did not fall into that category. As a result, Kenny found himself literally fighting to save his life and to save his ass for more than 18 years. Even though an excellent book called *A Promise of Justice* was already written by David Protess and Rob Warden detailing Kenny and his codefendants' odyssey through the Illinois justice system, this part of the story is worth retelling here.

Kenny is perhaps the least famous of the four men who were charged and convicted for the rape and double homicide of a young white couple in 1978 in Ford Heights, Illinois. This may be because Kenny is quiet and, without question, is the most low-key and introspective of the group. Or, it might be because upon his sensational release and exoneration of this crime, he just faded into a quiet middle-class life. For whatever reason, he is the least well-known. One thing is for certain though, he was the bravest.

Kenny Adams is 6-foot-2-inches of solid black marble. Handsome, distinguished and quiet, he could easily pass for a professional athlete or a successful commodities broker. To see him walking, all 140 pounds of his Husky dog, you would think he hasn't a care in the world. You would think that maybe he's some kind of movie star you don't quite recognize. You wouldn't think he's a guy who did eighteen hard ones for a double murder.

By virtue of reading this book, you have shown a more than academic interest in the plight of the wrongfully convicted. Perhaps you have just become involved in a loved one's quest for freedom. Maybe you are a new lawyer in the public defender's office or a student at a university. But whatever your interest or background, Kenny Adams is a person you should know. Kenny Adams is the poster child for the wrongfully convicted and, for that reason alone, he is worth examining.

In 1978, as you walked into the Cook County State's Attorney's inner-office at the Markham courthouse, there sat a scale inside the office door. When a defense lawyer inquired one day as to the purpose of the scale, he was told by an assistant states attorney that is where they weighed convicted defendants. When the defense lawyer asked why, he was told by the young white man, "We have a contest here, whenever we convict somebody of a felony, we weigh them. The first assistant who reaches a ton wins the contest." The defense lawyer replied, "That's interesting." The man continued, "Yeah, well, we like it. We call it 'nigger by the pound.'" The defense lawyer was shocked, but not surprised.

It was under that regime and mindset that "The Ford Heights Four" were wrongfully convicted for one of the most brutal rape-murders in the history of Cook County. Dennis Williams, Willie Range, Verneal Jimerson and Kenny Adams were the four young, African-American men whose own personal version of hell fell down squarely on top of them. Williams and Jimerson eventually received the death penalty, while Adams and Range received what amounted to life sentences.

In multiple trials, inept defense attorneys, perjured testimony and outrageous police and prosecutorial misconduct kept them in prison for over eighteen years. Their cases were a blueprint for what is now known as a wrongful conviction. Back then it was called a lot of things, from "getting screwed" to "getting fucked." But it was not called a wrongful conviction. Today we have cleaned up the language and the terminology. But if you're living it, the more sanitized term doesn't change a thing.

Having worked on what is now known as "The Ford Heights Four" case, I can say it was one of those experiences you would not believe unless you experienced it personally. If nothing else, it helped us learn what it takes to overturn a wrongful conviction. This book is based largely on those cornerstones. The team approach, the discovery, and the investigative issues, all those things served us well then, and they continue to serve us well in these types of miscarriages of justice.

At one point during Kenny's incarceration when he was visiting with his parents, he told them about one of the state's offers to testify against his codefendants. He told them that on numerous occasions he had been offered his freedom in exchange for what would amount to perjured testimony. After a moment, Kenny's mother looked at him and said something that ripped her heart right out of her chest. She said, "Kenny, if you have to come home under those conditions, we would rather not have you".

Now imagine that for a moment. For those of you who have even a passing acquaintance with the criminal justice system, you know how often those types of deals are turned down. They aren't. But Claudette Hurly didn't have to think about it. After crying herself to sleep hundreds of times, after multiple trials, after a thousand false hopes, Claudette Hurly did what she always did. She acted honorably. She acted against her own self-interest and that of her son's. She did what the entire Cook County State's Attorney's office could not or would not do, and that was "the right thing."

On May 11, 1978, in the early morning hours in Homewood, Illinois, Larry Lionberg and Carol Schmal were at a small gas station where Lionberg was working the midnight shift. They had recently become secretly engaged and were keeping each other company when three black males and a Hispanic male pulled up to the station.

On May 12th their lifeless bodies would be discovered in Ford Heights, one in an abandoned town house development and the other at a nearby creek. Both were shot in the head at close range. Carol had been gang-raped and left naked from the waist down. As Ford Heights was a 100% African-American community and Lionberg and Schmal were Caucasian, this case immediately became what is known as a "heater case." In other words, the entire law enforcement community of the southern suburbs of Chicago was outraged, the media was outraged, and the pressure was on. There had better be justice in this matter and it had better happen sooner rather then later.

Within hours the Cook County Sheriff's Police brought into custody and arrested Dennis Williams, Verneal Jimerson, Willie Range and Kenny Adams, all African-American males who lived near where the victims were found. They were between the ages of eighteen and twenty. Williams was the only one to have ever been arrested prior to this and it was only for juvenile property crime. The other three had never had any police contacts. This was hardly your usual band of cut-throat killers and rapists.

Local police (in Ford Heights) who worked in the black community scoffed at the arrests. They knew who the outlaws in the community were and these guys weren't even in the same league. Their outrage over the arrest of these four men was quickly answered by the Cook County prosecutors, who basically fired them from the investigation. Dissent would not be tolerated. Damn it, we got the bad guys and that is the end of that, facts be damned.

Speaking of facts, there were no fingerprints, no weapon, no witnesses, (there was some perjured eyewitness testimony), no bloodstains and no motive. Proceeds from the robbery at the gas station were not found at or around any of the defendants' homes. There were no confessions, no admissions, no nothing. Dennis Williams said it best when he was being interrogated at gun point (literally) and was shown a crime scene photo of Carol Schmal's body: "When I seen that she was white, I knew we were dead men."

Four months after the crime, in front of a white judge, with white prosecutors, and an almost an all-white jury (there was a lone African-American seated), The Ford Heights Four went on trial at the Markham branch of the Cook County courthouse. (The place where "nigger by the pound" was invented.) It should be noted that most murder cases in Cook County do not go to trial for a minimum of two years. Sometimes if the defendants are in custody, it can be as long as seven years. But, you know what they say, justice delayed is justice denied. That was not going to happen here with these defendants.

Two juries were impaneled, one for the men and the other for Paula Gray, a girl-friend of Kenny Adams who had been terrorized by the police and indicted for perjury. Paula would wind up spending seven years in prison, having her parental rights terminated and generally becoming as big a victim as the men, literally continuing to the time of this writing in 2004.

During the course of the trial in 1978, the usual recipe for disaster followed. Conflicted, inept, eventually disbarred defense lawyers, jailhouse snitches, perjured testimony, withheld exculpatory evidence, a pissed-off judge and an outraged almost all-white jury brought home the desired result: Guilty on all counts. Williams received the death penalty, while Adams got 75 years and Range got natural life.

Jimerson would not be tried for another seven years, and when he was, he received the death penalty, just like Williams. In 1985, Paula Gray was the only witness to testify at Jimerson's trial. The prosecutors did not disclose to the jury that her testimony was in exchange for murder charges in the same case being dropped against her.

It was neat, uncomplicated and simple, much like a modern-day lynching. The only thing missing was the white hoods.

In the interim, the real killers would go on to commit at least three more homicides that would leave a whole host of new victims and their families in their wake. This was justice "Chicago Style." I regret to inform you that not much has changed in the ensuing 25 years.

So, as not to bore you with the never ending appeals, retrials, hearings and so forth, the Ford Heights Four continued on the merry-go-round of justice for the next several years. It was not until their case was brought to the attention of Rob Warden, the publisher of the Chicago Lawyer monthly magazine that was the watchdog of the legal community. Warden, who had been a gigantic pain in the ass to the authorities over the years with his books and articles on corruption, became interested in and eventually convinced of The Ford Heights Four's innocence. This would eventually start the tidal wave of bad news (in the State's Attorney office) that would eventually free these four men.

Along with Warden, Northwestern University Journalism Professor David Protess brought his considerable talents to the table. Between the two of them, they virtually knew the who's who in the zoo of Chicago legal, investigative and media communities. They are sort of like E.F. Hutton, when they talk, people listen. Protess had gotten involved based on the promise he made to death row inmate Gervis Davis on the night of his execution for a crime which he was likely innocent. Davis had begged Protess to look into the matter of Dennis Williams, who he had befriended while on death row. Much to the state's dismay, Protess was a man of his word.

Throughout the next few months Protess and Warden worked their magic, without any funding at all, and they did what they did best. They got investigators, lawyers, students, family members and anyone else they could think of to work on the case, for free of course. Literally thousands of hours and thousands of dollars poured out of everybody's pockets as they feverishly worked on the Ford Heights Four case.

Certain influential newspaper and television reporters took up the cause by exposing the authorities' misconduct in the case. At lightning speed the case turned into a firestorm of bad publicity for the state. It was getting real hot in the kitchen.

To complicate matters further, Warden was now working as an executive officer and policy wonk for the then-current State's Attorney Jack O'Malley. The fox was literally in the henhouse and he was walking a real tightrope. O'Malley was not your average politician. He was a former street-smart tactical unit investigator for the Chicago Police Department who had gone to law school at University of Chicago (The Yale of the Midwest) while he was still a policeman.

O'Malley was very much aware of what was going on with the case. His office, then under Mayor Richard Daley, had prosecuted the case. When Daley was the state's attorney the office was notorious for wrongful convictions.

The holdovers from that era were not at all happy about being ripped in the news everyday. As with all of the other wrongful conviction cases, the office was maintaining that they were right and they had the right guys.

O'Malley was in a tight spot. His chief political advisor and executive assistant were telling him that they had the wrong guys in jail. His senior assistant state's attorneys were telling him no, they had the right guys. Everyone was maneuvering and taking sides. The price of poker was rising dramatically. O'Malley was leaning towards Warden's version. This was wreaking havoc on a major scale within the office. O'Malley was starting to think that maybe the police department wasn't such a bad place to be after all. In the end, Jack O'Malley would do the right thing. He paid with his political future.

After almost eighteen years when the boys could not buy a break, things were looking up. In jail they were the most famous inmates in the system. Hell, they were more famous then the damn Beatles were in Ford Heights. Suddenly there is a whole damn platoon of investigators, high-priced and free lawyers, and half the Chicago media was working, writing or talking about them. Things were definitely looking up. Talk about your out-of-body experiences, the boys were, as they say, cautiously optimistic.

Be that as it may, The Cook County prosecutors in the Markham courthouse were digging in. The hell with O'Malley and those assholes in the media, this was a war dammit, and we ain't caving in to a bunch of liberals and ghettoites. Nobody's getting out of jail just yet. Unfortunately for the boys down at the courthouse, the bad news was just starting. It would get worse.

And it did get worse, in the form of a cute, little Irish woman named Sheila Murphy. Now, if Sheila Murphy had just been a cute, little, middle-aged Irish lady, the prosecutors would have just written her off as another do-gooder liberal. But, once again, the gods had turned around and were smiling on the Ford Heights Four.

Sheila Murphy was a judge in the Markham courthouse and she just wasn't some political-hack judge, she was the Chief Judge, and as such wielded a whole lot of power. Sheila Murphy was also a former defense lawyer who had a long career and a longer memory of what kind of Machiavellian schemes went on in Cook County.

Judge Murphy came from the real school of hard-knocks. The daughter of a prominent trial attorney in Colorado, Judge Murphy was a schoolteacher and mother by trade when she decided to attend law school in Chicago. Nowadays, that might not seem like a big deal, but when Judge Murphy went to law school she was not only pregnant but one of only four females in the class. By the end of her first year of law school she would be the only female on the DePaul Law Review.

It was at law school that Judge Murphy started learning how things are done "Chicago style." At the law school Judge Murphy attended, it was routine for the top students to receive scholarships after their first year of school.

Judge Murphy was eligible but was told by the Dean that, "the scholarships are reserved for married men with families to support." Judge Murphy told the Dean that she was pretty certain there were laws against that sort of thing, as she was married and was helping to support a family as well. Judge Murphy was quietly given her scholarship.

After graduating from law school, Judge Murphy decided that she wanted to be a criminal defense lawyer. She attended an American Trial Lawyers conference with her dad and mom in Las Vegas and in that spirit wrote a letter to the Cook County Public Defender. In 1970, law firms were only hiring women as clerks or secretaries. The PD, having a sense of humor, hired her—you guessed it, as a juvenile public defender. You know, women should be with the kids and all that.

Fast-forwarding to the Markham courthouse twenty something years later, Judge Murphy was a force to be reckoned with. She had a reputation as a fair, no-nonsense judge, who played it straight. Her detractors, however, were numerous. Among them were judges in powerful positions, who were constantly setting her up to fail. When Judge Murphy became the Chief Judge at Markham, the place had the worst reputation in the county. Nobody had been able to bring order and discipline to the courthouse. The county was littered with the bodies of former Chief Judges who had tried and failed.

Judge Murphy was sent to Markham to fail. She was starting to gain a following among Chicago's more powerful Democratic politicians. Her detractors thought that if they dumped her in that "hellhole" she would be just another loser in an already long line of losers. Whoops, they didn't figure on Sheila Murphy's resolve and character. She not only turned it around, but also became even more formidable. Her reputation was skyrocketing.

Now as Chief Judge, Murphy could pick and choose what cases she heard. She assigned herself to the Ford Heights Ford case. Like everyone else in the legal community, Judge Murphy smelled a rat. She wanted to smell it herself before anything further happened that would come back to haunt one of her judges.

At this juncture the case was "the case" in Chicago. Four alternative suspects had been identified as the real killers. Three of them had confessed and the fourth was dead. Inside the courtroom a pitched battle was evolving. The Ford Heights Four were now represented by a who's who of the Chicago legal community. Gone were the drunken and disbarred attorneys who had previously represented them at trial.

The big boys were here now and the price of admission had definitely risen. Scott Arthur, who is now in private practice, represented the Cook County State's Attorney's office. It was Arthur who had put them in jail eighteen years earlier. Good and evil were being fought here. The race card was on the table and it was being prominently displayed. Careers were being made and broken. This was not a place where one wanted to lose. Too much was at stake. In the center of the storm sat Judge Murphy.

Most judges would have been looking for the nearest golf course. Not Sheila Murphy, she was sitting right where she wanted to be front and center. She had the best seat in the house.

While Dave Protess was on the front steps of the courthouse vilifying the State's Attorney's office daily, (you would have thought that Pontius Pilate was the prosecutor), and the lawyers were inside shredding the state's case, Kenny Adams was sitting in Menard quietly, until he was transferred to another facility in Danville, Illinois, in November 1988. Adams and his family were starting to see some light at the end of the tunnel. However, they were terrified of something else going wrong. It had been an unforgiving eighteen years and nobody was planning any parties yet, least of all the Adams family.

One of the big ironies in any wrongful conviction case is the fact that if you are accused of a horrific homicide(s), you are better off being accused of rape and homicide. The reason is fairly simple. In your run-of-the-mill homicide case, there is usually very little evidence that would help identify a perpetrator's DNA. However, in a rape case there are usually all kinds of body fluids available from victims' bodies that can help identify the actual rapist/killer.

In the Ford Heights Four case, they were fortunate to have been accused of a rape as well. As if the gods were still smiling on them, another miracle occurred. Actually, several miracles happened. First, the rape kits that were done on Carol Schmal were still in existence. Second, DNA testing had been born since the first conviction in 1978. When the guys were initially and again convicted several years later, it was the same Illinois State Police crime lab personnel that had identified Dennis Williams and Willie Range as the definite rapists of Carol Schmal.

Defense lawyers had been attempting to have DNA tests done for the last seven years. The state, for reasons known only to them, had successfully fought off the DNA tests. (This is a recurring theme that we see in these cases. The state just refuses to get the DNA done. When this happens, be leery.)

When Judge Murphy got involved she had the state do the test. However, this happened only after Paula Grey retracted her previous testimony. Judge Murphy told the state in no uncertain terms that their case against Verneal Jimerson was now without any evidence, and that they had better find some evidence or she would be forced to release Jimerson. In effect they only agreed to the DNA testing because they were desperate and out of evidence.

Finally, in 1996, Judge Murphy ordered DNA testing to be done at "the best lab" the lawyers could find. This was done only after the state was forced into an indefensible position. After samples were taken from the Ford Heights Four and the new murder suspects, everything was sent to Boston for Harvard Professor Dr. David Bing to analyze.

After testing the Ford Heights Four's blood samples, he found one right after another that the four men did not rape Carol Schmal. It was the first time ever that multiple defendants had been excluded by sources of semen in a rape case.

On June 14, 1996, the Ford Heights Four walked out of the main courthouse in Cook County at 26th and California in Chicago as free men for the first time in more than eighteen years. They had survived their own personal version of hell for more than eighteen years. They were exonerated. While incarcerated, cell phones, VCRs, remote controls and microwave ovens had come into existence. They were shocked by the bombardment of technology. Their senses were overwhelmed. They were now all grown men who had literally grown up in jail. They had no idea what the future held. They did know one thing for sure, they were going home.

Kenny Adams ordeal went way beyond just being "locked up." Every day and just about every hour, he lived with the thought of being able to free himself with one phone call. All it would have taken was for him to contact the state's attorney and agree to testify against the other three. The "deal" was always on the table. All he had to do was reach across and grab it. Kenny would think of how when he first got arrested his youngest brother was three-years-old. He would fondly recall him standing on the front seat of the car pretending to drive. Eighteen years later he was as big as Kenny. An entire generation had become adults while the Ford Heights Four and Kenny Adams were held hostage.

In 1997, the Ford Heights Four filed civil suits against the Cook County Sheriff's Office for "intentionally manufacturing false evidence" to convict them. The author had gotten Wyoming attorney Gerry Spence to represent Dennis Williams. Shortly after filing, Spence helped negotiate a $36 million settlement for the boys.

In April of 2003, the Ford Heights Four became one short. Dennis Williams tragically died in his home. He had some minor blockages in his arteries, but it was stress that took Dennis's life. The most outspoken and the angriest of the Ford Heights Four, Dennis never got over having his life stolen from him. Although not as angry as he once was, he was still very bitter. He appreciated his freedom like few Americans before him. His death was just another tragedy in a string of tragedies. The peace that so eluded Dennis in life is now his. He is terribly missed.

Kenny Adams got out of prison and conducted himself like he always did, with class, dignity and pride. He is now happily married, loving his life and freedom. The strength of character he displayed throughout his life is as strong as ever. It is that very strength that this country was founded on. It is the type of strength that allows all of us to continue this often thankless work in the face of overwhelming odds.

The Ford Heights Four affected all of us who worked on it in a way that is almost indescribable. All of us are better people for having worked on and successfully helped these men regain their stolen freedom. We learned many valuable lessons in overcoming impossible odds. But, what we learned most of all, is the importance of keeping and having heart.

Within the rest of this text we will provide you with hundreds of tricks-of-the-trade in dealing with wrongful conviction cases. Some of them will be very beneficial to you and your clients, some of them may not be.

In the end, if you take nothing else from this book, try and steal a little bit of Kenny Adams' spirit. Try and remember what kind of heart Kenny Adams had to possess in order to overcome his ordeal. If a little of Kenny Adam's heart creeps into your soul, you will be on your way to overcoming the wrongful conviction.

# 2

# *The Paper Trail & Case Management*

*"Take nothing on its looks; take everything on
evidence. There's no better rule".*

*—Charles Dickens*
*Great Expectations,* **40**

The history and of course almost any substantive evidence that you will deal with
in any old case will come from old discovery. Sometimes the discovery is complete. More often then not it is thrown into some cardboard boxes and left lying
around for years.

Occasionally, the client who has been sitting in prison for 10, 15, or 20 years will
have some of it. Finally, attorneys who have represented the client throughout
the years will have the vast majority of it. Well, at least hopefully the attorney will
have it.

Are you still with me here? The fact is that you will often be handed some of the
discovery most of the time, but in general you will almost never get all of the discovery every time. Transcripts, lab reports, appeals, prior investigative files, will
almost always be sorely lacking.

The first order of business in any old case is to assemble, locate and organize all
available discovery materials. This is much easier said than done. Often it turns
into a full-time job that will continue throughout your involvement in any specific case. It is a maddening, frustrating and never-ending quest. But, at the end
of the day, it must be accomplished.

The basic materials required should be, but are not limited to the following: *police reports, trial and hearing transcripts, appellate briefs, crime scene photos, transcripts of all 911 tapes that relate to the incident and/or the actual tapes, lab reports, technician and scientific notes that back up work product, relevant medical reports, pre-sentence reports, prison records, all crime scene investigation logs and inventory sheets, any and all photographs taken by police, lock-up reports, polygraph records, any demonstrative evidence used at trial, old timelines and people lists, defense investigative reports and all supporting documentation, prior expert reports used, any evidence depositions taken, attorney interview notes and anything else available or laying around.*

These materials are critical. Good luck getting a complete set, but you have to make the effort. When you have secured these documents, you are ready to start the fun part of the case. This consists of actually reading the material, digesting it, and then organizing the file.

## *People List*

When reading the never-ending discovery that will come at you all at once, or dribble in over several months, do yourself a favor. Start a people list day one. Save yourself a lot of grief and start writing down every name you come across. Do not delete anyone. Any name mentioned in a case file may be critical.

The basic premise is that you won't know who is critical when you start. You may think you do, but in reality almost every case that I have reviewed over the years had names/witnesses in it who the person prior to me considered insignificant or unimportant. Occasionally they were dead wrong.

The point is that you may discover something later that now makes that past unimportant witness critical. In addition, at some point you are going to have to account for every single individual who is mentioned in the case.

This is a lesson that was difficult to learn, because, like most of you, I find the paperwork boring. It may be boring, but as they say, the devil is in the details.

Fortunately for those of you reading this today, there are much simpler ways to accomplish this. When I first started in this business, you basically sat down and wrote out a list in longhand, dictated it or typed it. That method was time-consuming and repetitious. Now, due to modern technology, we have computer programs that sort it all out for us.

I use software called *Casemap 4*. It allows you to name and organize your own fields and it is amazingly simple to use. It will save you a lot of time and effort as the case progresses.

## Timelines

The timeline is simply a way to list all significant events that have occurred in any given case. Once again I use a software product that does all the work. All I do is plug in the data. The timeline shows what happened when and what individual was involved. Timelines are critical because they will often show conflicts in stories and evidence presented.

Generally the paralegal in the case is assigned to this task. However, whoever is reviewing all of the paperwork initially can at least initiate the timeline. As with the people list the timeline should remain fluid enough so that it can be changed frequently. The software I use is called *Timeline 3*. It is well worth your initial investment.

## Subpoenas

There is no more powerful tool available to the defense team then the old subpoena. If you have the ability to issue subpoenas never miss the opportunity to utilize it early and often.

Over the course of twenty five-plus years in this business, I am continually surprised at the lack of defense personnel who utilize this tool effectively. The reasons that they are underutilized are mind boggling. In that spirit, I will try to address their many uses here.

The basic purpose of a subpoena is to issue a written order of court, (the Judge in effect) that orders someone to appear in court to give testimony. Or, it is a written order of court to bring specific records or documents to the courthouse for examination.

In general, subpoenas are used to gather information, summon people to court, and bypass freedom of information requests. Judges are the ultimate ruling authorities on what may or may not be subpoenaed in a criminal matter.

It can be a very powerful tool that solves a lot of mysteries. It can be a tool that aggravates the hell out of a witness. Generally speaking, it is an intelligence tool used by both the prosecution and defense.

The issuance of a subpoena is done differently from jurisdiction to jurisdiction, which can be a maddening experience for those of us who work in multiple areas of the country. But, nevertheless, to be effective, you had better know the rules.

In the purest sense of the matter it is *the court*, who issues the subpoena. In other words, the court issues the subpoena, receives the person or information sought and decides as to whether or not the material or person received is relevant to the case in question. The court also determines whether or not the information should be released to the defense team.

I have seen courts that could care less what is being subpoenaed into court and they offer no interference in any way.

And I have seen courts who micromanage every subpoena issued. As with everything that we deal with in the criminal justice system, this makes little sense, but we have to learn how to manage and gather the information sought in a responsible manner.

Federal court is different from state or superior court. Superior court is different from county to county. So whatever the court's pleasure, you have to figure this part of the equation fast.

After you have dealt with this mystery, the Judge will no doubt create another rule that isn't on the books and further confuse the entire issue. It is at this juncture usually that you will realize just how much power the trial judge has in either thwarting your efforts or advancing your cause. This is a good spot to mention that as participants in these forays all we seek form the judge is one thing; A level playing field. Just give us the opportunity to get to the bottom. We don't need help, we don't require an advantage. Basically just leave us alone and quit cheerleading for the prosecution.

I am, of course, partial to the judge who leaves us the hell alone and allows us to seek anything that might be remotely beneficial to our latest cause. The state, of course, just hates our ability to legally meddle in their witness's confidential informant files, income tax returns, drug test results and other troublesome well-directed inquiries into the general character and disposition of their star witness(es).

If the defense attorney has been in a drug-induced stupor for the last several months this is where he or she must wake up and fight the good fight. As my own personal experience has taught me, prosecutors, although almost always under rules of "mutual discovery", will generally withhold whatever they deem beneficial to the defense.

If they did not, we would have no need to subpoena everything because the prosecutor would have provided it at an earlier date. Don't hold your breath waiting for that to happen.

I cannot begin to describe how often we have "gotten lucky" and subpoenaed relevant and critical documents that have saved the day, only to find out later the prosecutor had possessed the document(s) in question for months or years.

For instance, we have subpoenaed jail log records that have shown the local police visiting an "unbiased witness" twenty or thirty times prior to trial. What the hell did they talk about at all those visits? Generally they won't even disclose these visits, unless you catch them.

My rule of thumb for subpoenas in general is, when in doubt issue a subpoena. If the presiding judge has the good sense to let you truly investigate a case they will allow the defense to subpoena anything they want. There will always be a time later in the case where the judge can tell you "nice try," but that stuff is not coming in. The trick here is, if you're allowed to, issue the subpoena and worry about the relevant law later.

When subpoenaing documents always ask for the originals. If the originals aren't available get certified documents. When the information you are seeking isn't available or the agency or entity in question is denying its existence, obtain a sworn affidavit stating so.

## Subpoena Logs

In some cases we will have issued one or two hundred subpoenas. It's fairly simple and routine, but once again it will turn into a paperwork nightmare if you don't keep up with the "paper."

Subpoena logs are simply a detailed list of who the subpoena was issued to and when. When it's due back in court. Who received the materials requested.

Who is the contact person that is dealing with the subpoena and did they comply with the request. This is where the professional paralegal is invaluable. They generally have the expertise and know how to keep up with the paperwork.

## Trial Exhibits

While gathering all of this paper, occasionally a light will go off in your little head and you will decide this particular item will make an excellent trial exhibit. For some reason, trial exhibits seem to get little attention from the defense side of the aisle.

Before I get ahead of myself, I should probably explain just what an exhibit is. It is anything that will tend to cast a favorable light on your theory of the case. The following are excellent trial exhibits and should always be considered for the show-and-tell aspect of any trial or hearing.

- Crime scene photos.
- Transcripts showing prior inconsistent statements.
- Photos of physical evidence.
- Mug shots of hostile witnesses.
- Telephone records.
- Any official documents that support your theory or theme.
- Criminal records of witnesses.
- Relevant autopsy photos or reports.
- Relevant police reports or police notes.
- Relevant lab reports that support your theory.
- Crime scene sketches.

- Any evidence that shows or proves your client was abused, beaten or tortured while they were in police custody.

Basically anything that will impress a jury or trier of fact. Remember, big is better and really big is great. Don't be shy, blow up exhibits or PowerPoint them so that the judge or jury can see them clearly across the hallway.

The trick is to take over the courtroom and make it your home field. The government is a master at doing this. You should at least fight them to a draw on this issue. If you don't, you may lose before the first witness ever gets called to the stand.

### Client & Family Management

I don't know what the hell client management has to do with paper trail, but I didn't know where else to put this and so here it is. I hope you read it because it is truly critical.

Unfortunately, the defendant/client/mope of the day/lunatic/career criminal will be sitting in the courtroom every time there is a relevant hearing. Hopefully, it will be the client and not the other ones. However, clients being clients we really don't have a choice in the matter. We must be prepared to deal with the hand that we were dealt.

After many years I'm not sure what is worse: Scott Peterson or Charlie Manson? The Hillside Strangler or Ted Bundy? The Melendez Brothers or John Gotti? You tell me because they all wound up in the same place. So, whether or not your client has teeth, tattoos on his face, or model good looks, I'm not sure what works.

But I do know that if the client is not brought into the inner circle, advised properly, and given a steady course on what will do him in, he will generally self-destruct in front of the judge or jury. He can't help himself. He will do it every time. This part here is to help you to minimize the damage he will ultimately do.

I am a firm believer in involving the client as much as possible. If they feel involved, they feel empowered. If they feel like you're treating them like meat, they will fight you everyday and every hour. Not good, and not much fun considering that you already have plenty on your plate.

Personally, I like dealing with the career professional criminal. They know why they're here, and they know why you're here. They don't cry, complain or whine. They know the system as well as you do, and they don't sweat the small stuff. They don't bitch about jail food, visitations, and your legal or investigative expertise, (generally).

Often they are smart and they are on board with what you are trying to do. Just as often they are too smart and a genuine pain in the ass, but they are controllable as long as they believe you are fighting the good fight.

In my first come-to-Jesus meeting with any client I tell him or her what I expect of them. In short, my rules for making the defense team's lives palatable and less difficult then clients tend to are fairly simple:

- Do not discuss your case with any inmates.
- Do not speak to any government agents of any type.
- Do not say anything on the phone that you don't want to hear in court later.
- Try not to commit any felonies while out on bond or in jail.
- Abide by any bond conditions.
- Act like a gentleman or lady in court at all times.
- Do not get into staring contests with police, prosecutors or witnesses.
- Do not tamper with potential witnesses.
- At least temporarily retire from all gang activity.
- Do not write any letters that are not privileged in nature.

These are the basic requirements. There will be more as time goes on but, these are the mandatory ones. If they can't live with them, say goodbye, because they will eventually ruin you if you don't get control immediately.

I cannot stress this point enough. Let's face it, the prosecutor and the police generally believe you and your client are partners and you love each other. The client will screw you after thinking about it for oh, about three seconds. The press and the geniuses who are not involved in your case will skewer you at every opportunity. It's basically a lose/lose situation unless you get control of it now.

The family, friends and colleagues of the client are a close second to the above. They may be paying you, so they will have a lot of animosity towards you. Believe me, when that retainer check clears and they don't see their loved one walking out of jail victoriously they will turn into a grizzly bear that has just gotten a vasectomy without anesthetic.

Nevertheless, they must be dealt with. On rare occasion they will be an asset. Rarer still, they will be helpful and contribute to the defense. Your job is to keep them busy enough to help you manage the client and put on a good show for the judge or jury. The first order of business with the client and his family is to make them understand that you are not going to do anything illegal, immoral, or unethical.

Do not ever imply that you can bribe the judge, influence a witness, or are engaged to juror number six. Unless you want to become the client's cell mate in a very short time, you will walk the straight and narrow at all times. Talking about it, winking and nodding about something shady or sinister will get you locked up. Don't play with this, because you will get caught even if you are only appeasing him with a line of nonsense.

Family members are good window dressing. Well, at least most of them are. If Mom doesn't look and act like Ma Barker and Dad doesn't appear to be the head of the Columbian Cartel they are usually assets. The general rule of thumb is, the more apparent and obvious family support your client has, the more chance he has to appear to be a citizen.

For example, a packed courtroom of well-dressed and well-behaved relatives will generally start to affect most judges and juries in a positive manner. In a long trial this is critical. Psychologically, it works well. The trier of fact will start noticing all these people and he or she, or the jury, will start identifying with some of them—hopefully. They will also quickly notice and assume that the client can't be all that bad if he has this much family support. They can't help themselves. The longer this goes on, the more positive influence you gain.

The prosecutors mastered this concept long ago. If nothing else they will pack the courtroom with cops and other prosecutors. This sends a silent message to the judge or jury that this case is very important to us, and you had better do the right thing if you want our continued support. This game cuts both ways, so whenever possible pack the audience with supportive and serious faces. Packing it at closing arguments is pretty worthless. It has to be a consistent force throughout the trial.

Getting control of the paper and the client are two of the most critical issues in any wrongful conviction case. If you fail to do this early on, you are setting your case up for failure. Neither one of these tasks is fun or pleasant, but they are necessary. Do yourself and the team a big favor, make it a priority in your case.

# 3

## *The Team Concept*

*"Talk is cheap. It's the way we organize and use our lives everyday that tells what we believe in."*

—Cesar E. Chavez, 1927–1993

After having lived through mostly media-generated fairy tales about the lone college student or isolated journalist being responsible for the exoneration and eventual freedom of a wrongfully convicted person, I am happy to report that it never happens like that. Like Cesar Chavez said, "Talk is cheap." He was right. The reality is that in the dozens of wrongfully convicted cases in which we have been involved that have turned out successfully, it was the team effort that carried the day. Certainly there is almost always an individual that does something extraordinary in any given case, but the reality is that, without a concerted effort on the part of everyone involved, you will not succeed in righting your particular miscarriage of justice.

So who is involved in these efforts? Is more better than few? Moreover, who is in charge of this cluster nut? Well, all of these questions are critical. So we should start with: How is the team assembled and why/how does it get assembled in the beginning? If you are an inmate rotting in jail for a crime that you did not commit, we hope you are paying attention. Because, if the team is not assembled properly, you will likely die where you are sitting.

The Team is born: Here is the reality; you are on year seven of a fifty-year sentence for a crime of which you had no part. Because of a myriad of reasons such as police misconduct, misidentification, etc., you have been convicted and your subsequent appeals have been denied. Your family is poor, you are broke and basically nobody gives a damn. In other words, your prospects for attending next year's Super Bowl in person are slim. What do you do?

The first thing you do not do is give up. There are people out there who will listen to you. They may be attorneys, journalists or private investigators. It could be a professor at a local university. It may be just about anyone who cares about justice. But, it is going to be your job to find them. They generally will not seek you out. If they have a reputation for doing this sort of work, believe us when we tell you they already have plenty to do. You are not even on their radar screen. You need to think about whom you decide to choose before you do anything.

Writing letters to Johnnie Cochran, Gerry Spence, George Bush or your respective governor may make you feel better, but it's a waste of time. They get hundreds of letters a year from people like you. For the most part their eyes will never see them.

So quit with your favorite celebrity genius and start thinking about the person or persons who will at least listen. If you buy this book and reference it in your letter, we will at least answer your initial correspondence (I know it's a pitch for a sale, but at least we're honest).

So, what are you going to put in this letter? Well, let us tell you what not to put in it. If you put in more then one reference to God, the Higher Being, Buddha, Allah or any other religious figure, we will throw your letter out.

If you tell us how we will "get rich" with your civil case for wrongful conviction, your car accident or your medical malpractice case, we will throw the letter out. If you are a woman and you send sexy or nude photos of yourself, we will throw the letter out (Ciolino might keep the pictures, but the letter will still be thrown out).

If you send us a 22-page dissertation about your case, we will throw the letter out. If you write more than one paragraph telling us how great we are, we will throw the letter out. We already know how great we are. Don't insult our intelligence by kissing too much ass.

If the letter was written with any human waste material, crayons, notes outside the margin, you guessed it, out it goes. In summary, we care about your plight, but don't overdo it.

What we want in a letter is simple. Two to five pages, typed, and in some sort of logical order. We don't grade for grammar or spelling (clearly if you have read this far, you should realize that much). We want to know the basics and they are this: Where were you arrested and by whom? Who prosecuted the case? Who was/were your lawyer(s)? Were/are there any issues of torture? What are the basic facts of the crime you were alleged to have committed, i.e. who, what, where, when and how? It doesn't matter that you didn't do it. Tell us what was alleged. Tell us if any other agencies, individuals, etc., have helped you in the past. Send us the name of a relative that we can contact. In short, don't waste everyone's time with pleas for mercy. We'll have plenty of time for that later.

If we are interested, we will respond by setting up a meeting with you, your family or other interested persons/entities. If we are not, for whatever the reason may be, we will at least write you back with some hopefully helpful suggestions. In the end, keep it simple. The pity party is over and you need help. Think about this in a very serious manner. It may be your last chance for freedom. You are more likely to get more responses by using some common sense in your initial request for assistance. If you are a friend or relative of an inmate, the same rules apply.

Whatever the manner in which someone gained enough interest to take up your cause, a team has to take it on in order for a successful conclusion.

So, you now have written a letter or several letters and somebody has decided to take a look at your train wreck of a case. If it weren't a train wreck, you wouldn't be reading this. In any event, what happens next? The most critical aspect of any wrongful conviction case is simply the paper trail. We need transcripts, police reports, lab results and crime scene materials. We cannot operate without them. Initially, everything rides on you and your team's ability to gather the paperwork of your case. It is simply the roadmap to your eventual release. Without a complete set and careful review of your paperwork, the effort will be ineffective and futile. Failure is almost guaranteed.

We have told you (the client/inmate) how to get the team's attention. So now we have to tell you and the professionals reading this who should be on the team. Well, like the theme of the case, this also has to remain flexible.

We have worked with three people on a team and we have worked with twenty. More is not necessarily better. A number somewhere in between is manageable.

Whatever the number may be, there must be direction and leadership.

Often it is from an attorney who may be involved. Sometimes it is an investigator who has decided to take the case. Occasionally a college professor may have taken on the case as a class project. But whoever usually gets involved initially, that individual will set the tone and the manner in which everything gets accomplished.

Under the best of circumstances there is a huge budget for a wrongful conviction investigation. Money is no object and whatever the team needs, the team gets. Nonsense. This almost never happens. Generally there is no budget, or in plain English: The team is as broke as the inmate. This will cause a number of problems, the biggest being time and expenses. For the most part, the team is donating their time, effort and money.

This causes delays that are not always advantageous to the client, but they are unavoidable. Everyone involved in these efforts are sacrificing much. Patience and understanding of work schedules, prior commitments, personal obligations and such must be taken into consideration. All of these needs have to be considered when thinking about taking on the assignment. Often you and the team are working on a deadline. On the other hand, the client may not be going anywhere for several years, so no sweat. Of course he or she may have something to say about that schedule.

While we're on the subject of "The Client" we should address how the team goes about dealing with the client. We freely substitute client for inmate because, well, it sounds better and if we have a legal relationship with this person, he or she is, in fact, a client. For all practical purposes we do have a legal relationship with the client once we agree to take on the case. We may not always treat them like a free person who is walking into the office on a daily basis, but we should.

One of the single biggest problems with managing this particular client is the same as with "normal clients." A lack of communication or the failure to treat the person with respect and courtesy is not necessary, nor is it professional. When an individual is incarcerated, is broke, and is fairly hopeless, this is the time that he or she should be treated well. Remember that you volunteered. Just because this is pro bono doesn't excuse you from good manners and common decency.

Now, on the other hand, you may have had to, on occasion, deal with the client who acts as if he is the only client you have and a well-paying one at that. Ten collect calls a day and long rambling correspondences that he expects to be answered right now are commonplace. This is where client management is essential if everyone is to maintain his or her sanity.

The best way to go about this is to designate someone on the team to communicate with the client. Perhaps two people, but no more than that. The client, in all likelihood, will be able to offer some suggestions as to how to help the case. A bright, intuitive client is always welcomed. However, most of our clients fall short of this ability for a host of reasons. You have determined the best way to manage these ever-continuing problems. Limits must be set early and revisited often. Firm yet flexible control has to be maintained. Do not assign this task to someone who can't say "No!"

Assign it to the individual who has the most kids at home. They know how to say the word no and mean it. They know when to be helpful and are capable of really listening.

Seriously, the individual(s) assigned to this task have to be very mature and not the type that can be easily manipulated.

When these cases are initially undertaken, there is often no lawyer around. Sometimes that is a good thing. More often than not, it's a really good thing. Lawyers are very much like the client. They are often needy, ego-driven and in charge by birth or proclamation of the Queen. For the most part, at least in the initial stages of this inquiry, the attorney is unnecessary. There are exceptions of course. An example is when it is an attorney who is bringing the case to you. Obviously, it is then clear who is directing the play.

These comments are not an indictment against all lawyers. We have worked with the best and the brightest in the United States. It has been an honor to be affiliated with many of them. Having said that, we are often involved in these cases because of what the lawyer(s) didn't do or refused to do at trial. We would just advise everyone to proceed cautiously at this point.

This is also true when the case is brought to an investigator by an independent innocence project at a university or institution. Because they are bringing it to you, they often feel that they are in the best position to tell you what the investigation will entail or what you will or will not do. Time out. It is time to instruct you on the finer points of investigation.

Fact number one: No lawyer wins in court without great investigation. Facts are everything in these cases. Investigators gather facts. Not paralegals, not the lawyer's wife or husband, not the legal secretary and certainly not the college student working on the case. If you, as the litigator, want to win and win consistently, you had better get used to this idea.

Fact number two: Investigators gather information and facts. We are not the purveyors of fairy tales. We are often the bearer of bad news. We don't like it any more than you do. However, when we are delivering information that does not fit into the theme of the case, we are not at fault. There are a number of ways to attack bad news and overcome bad facts. Unless there is a string of bad facts to contend with, we can usually figure out a more creative way to overcome those issues. If everyone maintains their inner calm and thinks about the problem at hand, a solution can usually be found.

In cases where we have had a lot of success, there have been a number of professionals and amateurs involved working together as part of the team. This may sound easy at first blush. It is anything but easy. What it should be is a group of people who can put aside egos and reputations long enough to come to the assistance of an individual who has been severely screwed by the system. If there is a difficult part of this book to write, this is it. This is the part where critical analysis may sound like nitpicking or payback. It is anything but that. It is, in all actuality, an attempt to steer reoccurring problems that we have experienced from continuing to reoccur.

***The Students:*** In many wrongful conviction cases that we have undertaken, we have had the pleasure of working with young, bright and sometimes very talented students. Most of them are in a journalism or law school class. For the first time in their lives they are asked to do something that is totally out of their realm of experience.

They are asked to assist in saving an inmate's life. For the most part they respond in an enthusiastic and appropriate manner.

In some cases they try to become a part of the client's dilemma in an inappropriate and unprofessional way. They often become part of the situation for their own benefit by forgetting their original purpose of finding the solution to the predicament at hand.

It is easy to look upon issues with mature reflection. It is easy to see where things can and have gone wrong. It is quite another to avoid repeating the same mistakes. Students should be used in the following manner:

- Reading & doing case memos
- Courthouse research
- Helping maintain files
- Creating exhibits for court or press conferences
- Witnessing interviews
- Doing library or Internet research
- Participating in Brainstorming Sessions

Beyond the above areas, we would advise you to proceed very carefully when working with students. First and foremost, there is the issue of safety. When students start wandering around the ghetto or some other exotic location, there is the potential that they may become a victim. They are doing things that a civil jury, sitting in a courtroom, would definitely not consider part of the student experience. In other words, should they be injured or killed while out on this little sortie, you as the professor, along with your university, may be on the losing end of a multimillion dollar lawsuit. Don't cave into pressure from the students. You are in charge and thus ultimately accountable for their well being.

Some of the things that students should not be doing are:

- Interviews involving any critical witness
- Interviews where affidavits or sworn statements are to be taken
- Unsupervised jailhouse interviews
- Canvassing neighborhoods in high-crime areas

- Interviews with known felons or general bad guys

- Any interview alone or unsupervised

Students must never be left unsupervised. No "Lone Ranger" acts are to be tolerated. They should be made to understand that they do nothing without explicit permission and long discussion(s) prior to undertaking any aspect of the investigation. If they are unable or unwilling to live with your rules, say good-bye and say it quickly.

We generally enjoy working with students. They bring much enthusiasm and often a high degree of intelligence to the party. They are refreshing in their attitudes as they haven't yet become jaded or burned out. They care. They are eager to please and they are a wonderful source of free labor. Their reward is that they see and learn things that their peers never see or learn. They gain experiences that are invaluable in life.

In short, it is a win-win proposition for all. All that is required is common sense and close supervision.

***Paralegals:*** A good paralegal is invaluable. A bad one is better than nothing. Nevertheless, if you have a good one on the team, he or she will be worth their weight in gold. Paralegals are primarily used to keep the paperwork organized and in a useable manner. All good things eventually work their way into their area of responsibility. Find and keep the professional paralegal, you will not be disappointed.

***College Professors:*** The good ones are great, priceless resources. The bad ones will make your life miserable. If nobody else on the team is getting paid, at least they are.

They are great sources of funding and labor. They are bright, intuitive and helpful. They get it very quickly. They understand the dynamics of team play and they will generally go above and beyond the call of duty for the client. They usually bring the name of a well-respected university to the project.

***Family Members:*** They are often an enormous asset to the team. These people make the best guides. Like all good generals, the Wrongful Conviction team needs a scout or guide. The guide will help make introductions to people in the neighborhood who would otherwise be hostile. The guide of family member(s) has a vested interest in the outcome of the case. They will usually work very diligently for the right price…. FREE. The guide can often advise the team as to how to deal with racial or religious issues. The guide or family member can often overcome or short circuit any cultural differences that may not have been anticipated.

Then again there is the "Nightmare Guide." The Nightmare Guide often comes in the form of the spouse who met and married their spouse while he or she was incarcerated. Look out for this one. Far be it from the author to offer advice on marriage, however, with very few exceptions, (we're thinking more along the lines of none), run away from this team member. Reduce them to strictly clerical duties. Keep them away from any sensitive or potentially conflicting items. Never put your team or client in a position where this person or persons will have to testify. They would fall into the category of the prosecution's dream witness of the year.

*Mitigation Experts:* A good mitigation team member is priceless as well. Their expertise brings a different and unique perspective to the case. They concentrate on the client. They do the cradle-to-grave investigation of the client. They can often bring insight on to how best deal with the client.

*Other experts:* Crime scene, forensic animation, gunshot, fingerprint or DNA experts are often the linchpins to the wrongfully convicted client's journey. They should never be overlooked. In every case an expert or group of experts from every discipline should be sought.

*Attorneys:* Often the team will have more than one. As long as they understand their role within the framework (the legalities), there should be no problems. Usually someone takes responsibility for the grunt legal issues and the other one manages the case. If they don't know the difference, you will have your work cut out for you.

*Summary:* Every member of the team brings their own unique talents to the table. Some people are strong in paperwork, some have great people skills. Whatever their strengths, they all have a role to play in the successful conclusion of a wrongful conviction case.

# 4

## *The Case Theme*

*My soul, sit thou a patient looker-on*
*Judge not the play before the play is done:*
*Her plot hath many changes; every day*
*Speaks a new scene; the last act crowns the play.*

—*Francis Quarles, Epigram, Respice Finem*

In almost every wrongful conviction case that you encounter you will see that the single biggest problem that got your client convicted in the first place was a lack of a theme. Or if there was a theme it was abandoned or so convoluted that the message was lost. The theme is nothing more then a well-orchestrated play. There are a number of ways to avoid straying from the script when the case is revisited.

The first lesson is that the theme must remain fluid. There can also be a number of themes present, but the message must be geared towards a main theme. So what are the possible themes? Listed below are some starting points.

Remaining fluid is key. Let's face it, everybody brings a whole mess of bias and shitty life experiences to the table. This is why the theme has to be developed via committee. The attorney, investigator, family members, litigation person, jury consultant, the insurance broker from next door, they all have an opinion. In criminal defense circles there are only six basic themes. They are;

1.  Didn't happen, wasn't involved.

2.  It happened, but I was in Toledo on that day.

3.  It happened, but it was an accident.

4.  It happened, I was there, but I didn't know it was going to happen.

5.    It happened but I was incompetent, i.e. legally handicapped.

6.    It happened, and I had to do it. A.K.A. misdemeanor murder or public service homicide. Pray that finder of fact sees it your way.

Out of the six basic themes come the sub-themes. This is where one has to be careful. You cannot go about this in a scattered and senseless way. Think about what the state's response is going to be to your theme.

Examine all worst case scenarios, no matter how farfetched. You must have a well thought out plan to retort to the state's scenario.

Quite often your main theme will change. We have been involved in cases where the defendant was clearly incompetent. As a result that was our initial theme. However, upon further investigation, we discovered that the defendant was actually innocent. We then abandoned the incompetence theme and concentrated on the "he didn't do it" theme.

Of course good investigation will quite often force you to keep changing the theme. That is why it is important to never get married to one particular theme.

### *Innocence*

In any wrongful conviction case this will always be the main theme. It all starts with "my guy is innocent, he didn't commit this crime and he needs to be released right now." In a wrongful conviction case, this is always the main theme. If you abandon it or steer away from it you will be lost before you begin.

Innocence rolls off the old tongue quick. It's pretty easy to throw that bomb out there, but there will only be a couple takers. One of them will not be the prosecutor. It won't be the trial judge who heard the case and it won't be the cops who made the arrest. The innocence defense is without doubt the hardest sell you will ever attempt.

Contrary to folk myth and fantasy, we believe that the people on the defense side of the aisle are the toughest critics of this defense. Granted, they aren't going to be as upset as the state, but we as a group have way too much experience with our clients to just swallow his or hers claim of innocence. We as a group are our toughest critics. We are usually the second to last group to jump on the innocence bandwagon.

For those of you who are incarcerated and are reading this from your cell or prison library, we have a message for you: If you are truly innocent and you were wrongfully convicted, we care about your plight. Our colleagues and I will make every sacrifice to help you regain your freedom. For those of you who are thinking that this is another scam in a long string of scams, and that you will convince us of your innocence, we would caution you against this strategy.

We have met you and the results have been disastrous for you. We will figure it out. When we figure it out you will not be happy. There will be a whole bunch of folks involved in your plan that don't enjoy a legal privilege with you. In other words there will be a feeling of loss and betrayal. This in turn will cause them to say really bad things about you and perhaps seriously jeopardize any slim chance that you may have had at regaining your freedom. This plan is a very, very bad idea, and we would not recommend the playing of this card unless it's for real.

When reviewing a file for innocence the following investigative steps are highly recommended:

- Review entire transcript.
- Review all police, lab reports & crime scene data.
- Conduct in-depth interview with inmate/client.
- Carefully review and compare witness trial testimony with police reports.
- Contact police report witnesses who didn't testify. Why not?
- Interview all media personnel who wrote, reported on case. Obtain old media accounts.
- Interview friends, family and other advocates.
- Attempt to interview police personnel who have retired, quit or left law enforcement. Get impressions, you never know.
- Look for motive. Why this client?
- Staff with professional colleagues for their impressions.

### Staffing

As a team there will be no better way to critically look at your theme or investigative plan than to staff it. Generally we have been involved with efforts that involved as little as three people and as many as thirty. Depending upon the size and specific expertise of any given team, this may be the most critical aspect that will happen prior to investigation, court, or any other proceeding.

After the discovery has been broken down and read by everyone there should be a meeting that includes all the team members. At this meeting there should be a general consensus of what the issues are, and what is the most vulnerable part of the government's case.

At this point, if the team is large enough they should be broken up into smaller groups, where they will come up with an action plan on their own. The action plan is simply their ideas as to what should be done to accomplish whatever the team is trying to successfully attack.

After the smaller teams have done that, another meeting should be held and everyone will put their ideas on the table. It is at this juncture that the entire team will critique the smaller teams' ideas and discard the impractical and unnecessary.

What is left is the best plan available at that time. It is at this point that you have formulated your plan and decided on a course of action. This is critical to any long-term success that you may enjoy. It is time consuming, but it is extremely important in time management and cohesive efforts towards the eventual goal.

Past experience has taught us that the single biggest issue in any case is the ability to manage time and budget. All too often we have seen team members go off on wild goose chases that were ineffective and a waste of resources. Staffing the issues early and often should avoid this problem.

### *Police & Prosecutorial Misconduct*

Lets face it, murder cases are vastly overrated as being the most difficult to solve. What they are is emotionally-charged dramas where the stakes are the highest. As such, society, and Americans in particular, are always looking for a quick fix. Murder cases are often whodunits. In other words, why in the world would somebody want to kill this victim? Such, rampant speculation as to who is often misguided and based on one investigators instinct. This is where disaster started percolating for your wrongfully convicted client.

The manner in which people become law-abiding regular citizens one day and homicidal maniac murderers the next is a police-generated phenomena. As criminal defense professionals realize, bad guys evolve. They don't wake up at 42-years-of-age and decide to kill their eight-year-old daughter. But what they wind up becoming is an attractive target to law enforcement. They become the focus when immediate answers are not forthcoming.

Because we live in an age of instant gratification we have become used to instant results. Fast food, digital communications, supersonic air travel, etc., the world keeps moving at a faster pace daily. As a result, the general public and the press want answers yesterday. The police and prosecutors in a rush to get on TV and become famous want to accommodate all of these entities. A rush to judgment is almost always that recipe for disaster for your client.

When this happens the misconduct, incompetence and shenanigans that occur often result in the railroading of your client straight into the penitentiary. In the vast majority of wrongful conviction cases that we have examined this is the single biggest issue/cause of the wrongful conviction.

Preliminary investigative steps to be considered when looking at this issue are:

- Compare police testimony with police reports.
- Background police personnel, both civil and criminal
- Contact other professionals in defense community for opinion on police personnel.
- Do media search on involved police personnel.
- Verify client allegations of physical abuse, if any.
- Check workman comp. records for mental disability claims of involved police personnel.
- Check reputation, i.e. corruption rumors

### *Identification Issues*

When the police and prosecutors are behaving themselves and not committing felonies or manipulating evidence, this is the second leading cause of cancer, as they say. More men have been sent to prison on bad ID's then any other single cause. Throughout history and thousands of scientific studies we now know that the bad ID is the second leading cause of death for an innocent client.

How many sexual assault victims have gotten on a witness stand and sworn that the defendant was the rapist. "I recognize him because he lay on top of me as he raped me." "I'll never forget his face." Fast forward five, ten years later and a DNA test clears the defendant and the victim admits, "Well maybe I was mistaken."

Anyone who is honest and has given any thought to this issue will admit that in times of high stress or trauma people have a tendency to become somewhat excited. The adrenaline kicks into warp speed, and your body chemistry drastically changes. These instant violent reactions to your system wreak havoc on your central nervous system and brain. As a result, you are, for lack of a better term, a wreck.

To act rationally and think in a cognitive manner is almost asking the impossible. Delta Force Commandos, Navy Seals, and the like who train for years under the most stressful of conditions have a hard time maintaining their equilibrium when all hell breaks lose. Can you imagine how a soft civilian-type will respond? Well, most prosecutors would have you believe that a 70-year-old wheelchair-bound man in poor health would actually make a great witness to a highly-charged violent event. Or that a patrolman in a squad car at 2 a.m. is a trained professional observer, who through his many years of professional experience would not make a mistake on an ID in 1.3 seconds of observation.

The criminal defense professional knows exactly how reliable witness ID's are, and for that reason this must always be a consideration when thinking about your theme.

Preliminary areas of investigation should include:

- If lineup was involved obtain pictures of lineup participants.
- Possible links of witnesses to victim, police, client.
- Background all witnesses, including friendly ones. Determine physical and emotional issues.
- Always check and verify eyesight issues.

- Determine under what circumstances the ID was made.

- Determine how and when witnesses appeared and were located.

- Determine if contact between law enforcement and witness occurred prior to "real" ID.

- Determine whether or not witness has ever been a witness before.

- Evaluate witness testimony by reenacting circumstances.

## Informants & Jailhouse Snitches

If there was ever an issue or theme that could not be attacked as early and as often as humanly possible, this one is it. There is nothing lower then a snitch or a jailhouse informant. They will and have sold their Mothers down the river for a break in their sentence or those famous forty pieces of gold.

Jailhouse informants have been around since Biblical times. They are motivated by one thing and one thing only: How will this benefit me? How will I get my sentence reduced? How will it curry favor with the authorities if I help them? How can I screw my old partner in crime? How can I get even with somebody I don't like? The reasons are endless in their minds. The fact of the matter is that they will say or do anything to save themselves.

The only people that like informants and jailhouse snitches are the police and prosecutors. Well, they like them until they turn on them. Then they feel about them like you do—lying pond scum. Up until they turned they are just people "who have seen the error of their ways." Misguided, misjudged, and misunderstood is what they are before they turn on the hand that has been nurturing and taking care of them.

But, for the purposes of your theme, they are a gift from Heaven. They are almost always in an indefensible position.
They are unable to justify their actions and are such an easy target. If you find that your client is in a position to utilize this theme, don't blow it. Play this card early and often.

Preliminary investigative steps should include:

- Conduct extensive backgrounds in every conceivable jurisdiction.

- Always obtain jail log visiting slips/information.

- Obtain all previous incarceration records including: cellmate lists, psychological/psychiatric records, intelligence, diplomacy records.

- Obtain all previous legitimate employment records.

- Interview all former spouses, significant others.

- Obtain all law enforcement monetary rewards.

- Obtain copies of written prosecutor deals.

- Interview past victims.

- Interview any former law enforcement personnel who had prior dealings with snitch as either arresting officer or handler.

- Obtain all previous sworn testimony in any case.

- Obtain all booking photos.

### *Junk Science*

This subject would and will often fall under police and prosecutorial misconduct. However, we are now seeing so-called experts acting on their own agenda and lying to those who employ them, the prosecutors. Junk science has been around since prosecutors figured out that when you don't have a case, call an expert. Let him or her explain to the trier of fact why your defendant is guilty.

As a result the junk science experts are quickly becoming a more serious cause of wrongful convictions. Prosecutors long ago discovered that when you don't have a witness, and you don't have physical evidence and you really should not have brought this case to trial in the beginning, call Dr. Quack Quack. Dr. Quack Quack will explain to those simple bastards on the jury why this guy is guilty.

He will explain how this defendant was so slick as to outsmart the entire police department for so long. Dr. Quack Quack explains all. Dr. Quack Quack has scientific instruments that only he can understand. Dr. Quack Quack can explain away your clients alibi, his blood type, his DNA. Whatever the issue, Dr. Quack Quack has a theory and reason.

Making junk science one of the main themes of your case is a fairly straightforward proposition. The science was either good or bad. Usually when it's bad, it's very bad.

This is generally a tough area to investigate. First off, you are usually dealing with scientists and state or county employees. Throw in the fact that the scientist may also be a sworn agent or police officer and you have just entered the twilight zone of investigation where things are never as they seem.

As you will see later in the junk science chapter, sometimes it takes years for the junk science to come to the surface. If the individual in question was not part of the law enforcement apparatus, then you may be dealing with an outside expert who regularly testifies for the government. This individual often has a financial motive to testify, i.e. the state is his biggest customer, or he or she just may be on a mission to help remove the criminal element that plagues the community.

Investigative suggestions:

- Find out if lab is certified.
- Obtain past inspection results.
- Obtain budget records.
- Detailed background investigation on involved personnel.
- Obtain professional papers or past presentations.
- Attend any future presentations.
- Obtain academic or training and seminar records.
- Obtain record of outside payments from different jurisdictions.
- Obtain any Internet information.
- Post inquiries on Internet list serve's for other info.

### *Ineffective Assistance of Counsel*

For some reason the appellate courts love this issue when they are overturning a wrongful conviction. At least they did until they realized what a problem it was. Now, unless trial counsel was drunk, asleep and ineffective you will not usually win on this issue alone. But, the fact of the matter is that when you are looking at a potential wrongful conviction case and any of the reasons that we are exploring here were not addressed at trial, somebody was ineffective.

Mostly attorneys are ineffective in what they don't do. We believe that most lawyers take this business of their clients' freedom very seriously. However, what happens is that they are outgunned, outspent, or outworked by the other side. When this happens, ineffective assistance of counsel becomes a burning issue. Assuming that trial counsel really did try his or her best. Assuming that they really cared about their professional performance, and assuming that they had some degree of knowledge in these matters, this does not make one automatically effective.

Being ineffective comes in many different shades and colors. Sometimes trial counsel was handcuffed by the trial judge. Sometimes they were just very inexperienced. But mostly it was a combination of things. Whatever the cause, this is often a theme in your wrongful conviction case. It is one that should never be overlooked.

Investigative areas of consideration:

- Professional reputation and experience issues.
- Past track record in similar cases.
- Determine financial assistance provided to defense, i.e. experts, investigators, etc.
- Review transcript carefully.
- Determine past disciplinary complaints if any. Interview complainants.
- Interview appellate attorney. Get opinion on trial performance.
- Determine conflict of interest issues. i.e., representing co-defendants, past representation of witnesses, etc.
- Determine client contact, how frequent, when, where, etc.
- Interview and find out about relationship with client, before, during and after.
- Get opinion as to what he or she felt the best defense was and why.

### False Confessions

When we were young investigators, we always thought that when we heard the words, "he confessed to the crime," we were done. Case closed. Let's move onto the next case. Well, now that we are older investigators and we have seen much more then we did when we were younger, we have discovered something: Confessions by your client are not the end of the world.

A confession, as they say, isn't what it used to be. We now know that people falsely confess for a myriad of reasons. Physical torture, psychological manipulation, promises made, mental incapacity, all of these play a part in false confessions.

The general prosecution myth that people don't confess to crimes that they didn't commit has been shown to be just that, a myth. People do falsely confess and they do it for any number of reasons.

When a confession is the only evidence keeping your client in a correctional facility, this issue should be explored with as much diligence as required.

Investigative areas of consideration:

- How was confession obtained? Oral, written, recorded, videotaped, etc.
- Where was confession made or taken at?
- What happened prior to confession?
- Are there Miranda issues?
- Was client clean and sober?
- Was anybody other then sworn law enforcement personnel involved?
- Are there any issues of inappropriate physical misconduct?
- Interview any medical personnel involved in treatment at or near time of alleged confession.
- Are there any third parties who were present at time of alleged statements?
- Does client have history of law enforcement cooperation? Has client confessed before in other cases?

## *Judicial & Jury Misconduct*

For those of you who are just coming out of law school this theme may be difficult. For those of you who have tried more then two cases in your stellar and distinguished legal career, it will ring very true. Judges and juries blow it and they blow it often. The trick, of course, is proving it.

The first area on inquiry when this is suspected should always be the judge.
How do we know when a judge acted inappropriately or illegally? Well, trial counsel is usually the best judge of that. (Tongue-in-cheek.) Trial counsel will often smell that rat before his or her client gets screwed. If they are fairly certain of it, they will usually bring it up on the record. (You know the document you read before you committed to this case.) If it wasn't on the record they will have probably told someone in the legal community about it.

If and when it does come up, you had better be damn certain that before you yell about this allegation of judicial misconduct you are right. Because, if you are wrong Judge Jones will make it his life work to destroy you and your pitiful career. Now we suspect that just writing about this blasphemy and business about bad judges we will not help make a lot of friends who wear black robes.

Most judges are politicians. Like politicians everywhere they have usually sold a little bit of their soul to get elected. Like any elected official that you have ever encountered, judges are not exempt from the pressures of elected office. They have to raise money to get elected. They have to keep the media relatively happy. Above all, they had not better piss off the state's or district attorney more then once or twice a millennium. In other words, they had better play ball or suffer the consequences.

With little doubt we will one day be sitting on a witness stand in some distinguished jurist's courtroom. At that point while we are waxing eloquently about our investigative prowess, we will be confronted with this part of this book. And, Prosecutor Smith in his most saintly voice will say:
"Sir or madam, isn't it true that you have compared Judge Jones here with common pimps and car thieves?" (All the while playing to the jury with indignation, the message being, this investigator has insulted our fine judge.) And the author would reply in a straightforward and honest way, "Why no sir, I was talking about judges who have already been convicted and sent to prison for corruption." Prosecutors being prosecutors would then say, "Well then to whom were you referring to if not Judge Jones? And we would say well, how about Judge John J. Devine who got 15 years for racketeering and mail fraud, and Presiding Judge Richard F. LeFevour who got 12 years in prison for bribery, mail fraud and racketeering, or Judge Wayne W. Olson who got 12 years for throwing a murder case for a $10,000 dollar bribe. Do you mean those judges Mr. Prosecutor?"

The point of this entire theme is not to ignore it as pure fantasy or mere speculation. All of the aforementioned judges were tried and convicted for those crimes. When the rumors first surfaced nobody believed it. Well, history has shown judicial misconduct does happen. It happens more then one would like to believe it.

Insomuch as jury misconduct is concerned, it is more likely to happen then judicial misconduct. Threats to and harassment of fellow jurors, bribery, etc., have all been known to happen during jury deliberations. We interviewed a juror who spoke of a fellow juror who was an off-duty police officer that pulled a gun out during deliberations.

We have seen jurors have romantic relationships with prosecutors and conceal them from the court. In short, we have seen jurors commit as many crimes as our clients. Judicial and jury misconduct should never be overlooked as a possible theme in your wrongful conviction case.

Investigative areas of inquiry:

- Interview all jurors including alternates?
- Was there any harassment, threats, or overzealous arguments during deliberations?
- Did the bailiffs act responsibly? Legally?
- Was there any prior discussion of evidence, guilt, innocence, etc.?
- Were any voir dire questions testified to falsely?
- Background all jurors.
- Were all jurors following rules? Any media violations?
- Were their any hidden potential conflicts?
- Was there any inappropriate behavior or contact?
- Check judicial inquiry board for past disciplinary actions?

### *Political Prosecutions*

Historically, the Unites States has been the least likely country where a political prosecution has taken place. It happens, but not nearly as often as the other reasons stated here. Then again that position may well be judged by whether or not you are reading this from the bowels of some penitentiary.

For that reason and more, political prosecutions do happen. The American Indian Movement, the Civil Rights Movement, and other groups have all had members prosecuted for strictly political reasons. With the enactment of the Homeland Security Act, we will see more political prosecutions. With that in mind this is always a possible theme.

Potential areas of investigation:

- Was client member of any subversive group?
- Do freedom of information requests.
- Is client active in any groups that advocate government overthrow?
- Obtain book, newspaper, and magazine articles on group.
- Find out true measure of clients participation

## *Summary*

There are, as chronicled above, any number of themes that may be utilized in a wrongful conviction case. They are by no means a complete list of themes. You are only limited by the facts of your particular case. Generally it is a combination of any number of the aforementioned areas. But whatever your theme, the one constant is, "My guy is innocent, he didn't do it and he should be given relief immediately."

If you stray from that message, if you get bogged down in details when you are trying to maintain your theme, your team will lose focus. If the team loses focus, you will lose valuable time and resources that you can ill-afford to lose. We will guarantee one thing: If the theme gets lost in the details, your client will lose his life or freedom permanently. Always maintain your theme and focus. It will never let you down.

# 5

# Revisiting The Crime Scene Investigation

*By the sympathy of your human hearts for sin ye*
*shall scent out all the places—whether in church,*
*bedchamber, street, field, or forest—where crime*
*has been committed, and shall exult to behold the*
*whole earth one stain of guilt, one mighty blood*
*spot.*

Nathaniel Hawthorne, Young Goodman Brown [1835]

Whenever we give a speech to civilians or non-industry personnel, we are always asked about the television series CSI. Our response is always fairly standard: "The best fiction show ever made" or "That's a fabulous fairy tale." Because you see, we're still waiting for our first encounter with a crime lab that either has the same budget that the TV series has, or that actually has personnel who are really that competent. When one of you run up on a crime scene that was worked the way that it's worked on CSI, call us. We'd really love to see it in real life. Hell, we'd love to just read about it.

The actions of the investigating officers at the onset of an investigation at a crime scene can make or break the case years later. If they are cautious and methodical in the collection of evidence and the identification of potential witnesses, crucial evidence will not be lost or tainted forever. Quality crime scene investigations, or even consistent national standards, are fairly nonexistent at the time of this writing.

Great or superior crime scene workups by the police are as rare as finding a leprechaun. As a result, we believe that the failure to closely reexamine a crime scene by defense personnel should be a class X felony. It is rare indeed when we have revisited or reviewed a worked-over crime scene and found it to be a mistake-free area. There are almost always all kinds of reasonable doubt laying about waiting to be discovered. Your job is to find enough of it to terrorize the state's case in **chief**. This shouldn't be too difficult.

## Primary Crime Scenes

Unless your crime scene is in the middle of the Pacific Ocean you will have to leave that comfortable chair and cool fan blowing on you and actually go out and do some detecting. In between the time that you become aware of it and in between those $6 lattes, you need to go to your crime scene and move around it. We say this tongue-in-cheek, but it has been our mind-boggling experience that in many of the cases we reviewed nobody on the defense team actually went to the purported crime scene.

We know that most folks think that you can sit in front of that whiz bang, ultra fast computer of yours and solve all manner of crimes, but really, we are begging you, go to the crime scene and start verifying or disproving reported information.

Just because the crime you are investigating happened fifteen years ago doesn't translate into you ignoring the crime scene. When you are dealing with a potential wrongful conviction case all sorts of little plots and conspiracies have been percolating for years. The biggest place where data and facts get manipulated is usually at the crime scene. Buildings and obstructions magically appear and disappear. Nonexistent alleys and past construction sites appear. This is where what we call "result-orientated investigation" is developed and nurtured.

Result-orientated investigation is when the police have a certain set of facts that are indisputable. This is usually a good thing. The problems start appearing when these facts don't fit your client's activities or actions. This is when witnesses develop X-ray vision, can see 250 yards in the dead of night, and obstructions become nonexistent. This is normally due to poor planning on their part and what is commonly known in legal circles as "failure to investigate" on the defense team's part.

Crime scenes are not magical places. They are street corners, highways, convenience stores, parking lots, orange groves, homes, yards, etc. They are places that you hopefully have some life experience with. Before we can have a criminal act we have to have a place where it occurred. Sometimes there are multiple crime scenes. Such as we had in The Ford Heights Four case that was discussed in Chapter One. We have the gas station where the robbery and kidnapping took place and the abandoned town home where the rape and murder occurred. Finally we had a creek area where the second murder took place. Careful investigation of what was testified to at trial, and what was actually possible to have happened at those crime scenes were proven to be outright lies and perjury 18 years later.

Now, in that case, as in many other wrongful conviction cases in which we have been involved, the police had certain undeniable facts they had to deal with. Their problem quickly became one of forcing and manipulating trial testimony and statements to fit the known facts. After some preliminary detecting we were able to ascertain that much of what had been testified to was false, if not downright impossible. Had this preliminary and basic chore been done at the pretrial stage and not some seventeen years later perhaps the Ford Heights Four would not have been convicted to begin with.

## What Should Happen at the Crime Scene

You can almost always predict what the police investigation will be based on what happened after they gained control of a crime scene. If the crime scene was handled with care and a manner consistent with the preservation of critical forensic evidence, then the later stages of that particular investigation may follow suit.

However if the crime scene was "trashed" and handled in a way that is inconsistent with acceptable forensic standards then the rest of the investigation was probably conducted in a similar fashion. A careful review of police-generated reports will normally reveal which scenario was followed.

The acronym KISS (keep it simple stupid) should be the golden rule when police agencies approach a crime scene. This is not neurosurgery. It is the preservation, collection and the safeguarding of physical evidence. With that in mind the Unites States Department of Justice published a guide called Crime Scene Investigation. What follows verbatim is some of their excellent advice.

## Initial Response/Receipt of Information

***Principle:*** One of the most important aspects of securing the crime scene is to preserve the scene with minimal contamination and disturbance of physical evidence. The initial response shall be expeditious and methodical. Upon arrival, the officers shall assess the scene and treat the incident as a crime scene.

*Policy:* The initial responding officer(s) shall promptly, yet cautiously approach and enter crime scenes, remaining observant of any persons, vehicles, events, potential evidence and environmental conditions.

*Procedure:* The initial responding officer(s) should:

a.   Note or log dispatch information (e.g., address/location, time, date, type of call, parties involved).

b.   Be aware of any persons or vehicles leaving the crime scene.

c.   Approach the scene cautiously, scan the entire area to thoroughly assess the scene and note any possible secondary crime scenes. Be aware of any persons and vehicles in the vicinity that may be related to the crime.

d.   Make initial observations (look, listen, smell) to assess the scene and ensure officer safety before processing.

e.   Remain alert and attentive. Assume the crime is ongoing until determined otherwise.

f.   Treat the location as a crime scene until assessed and determined to be otherwise.

*Summary:* It is important for the initial responding officers to be observant when approaching, entering and exiting a crime scene.

## Secure and Control Persons at Scene

*Principal:* Controlling, identifying and removing persons at the crime scene and limiting the number of persons who enter the crime scene and the movement of such persons is an important function of the initial responding officer(s) in protecting the crime scene.

*Policy:* The initial responding officer(s) shall identify persons at the crime scene and control their movement.

*Procedure:* The initial responding officer(s) should:

a.  Control all individuals at the scene-prevent individuals from altering/ destroying physical evidence by restricting movement, location and activity while ensuring and maintaining safety at the scene.

b.  Identify all individuals at the scene such as:

   • Suspects: Secure and separate

   • Witnesses: Secure and separate

   • Bystanders: Determine whether witness, if so treat as above, if not, remove from the scene

   • Victims/family/friends: Control while showing compassion

   • Medical and other assisting personnel.

c.  Exclude unauthorized and nonessential personnel from the scene (e.g. law enforcement official not working the case, politicians, and media).

*Summary:* Controlling the movement of persons at the crime scene and limiting the number of persons who enter the crime scene is essential to maintaining scene integrity, safeguarding evidence and minimizing contamination.

## Boundaries: Identify, Establish, Protect and Secure

*Principals:* Defining and controlling boundaries provide a means for protecting and securing the crime scene(s). The number of crime scenes and their boundaries are determined by their location(s) and the type of crime. Boundaries shall be established beyond the initial scope of the crime scene(s) with the understanding that the boundaries can be reduced in size if necessary but cannot be as easily expanded.

*Policy:* The initial responding officer(s) at the scene shall conduct an initial assessment to establish and control the crime scene(s) and its boundaries.

*Procedure: the initial responding officer(s) should:*

a.  Establish boundaries of the scene(s), starting at the focal point and extending outward to include:

   • Where the crime occurred.

- Potential points and paths of exit and entry of suspects and witnesses
- Places where the victim/evidence may have been moved (be aware of trace and impression evidence while assessing the scene)

b. Set up physical barriers (e.g., ropes, cones, crime scene barrier tape, available vehicles, personnel, other equipment) or use existing boundaries (e.g. doors, walls, gates).

c. Document the entry/exit of all people entering and leaving the scene to maintain integrity of the scene.

d. Control the flow of personnel and animals entering and leaving the scene to maintain the integrity of the scene.

e. Effect measures to preserve/protect evidence that may be lost or compromised (e.g., protect from the elements (rain, snow, wind) and from footsteps, tire tracks, sprinklers).

f. Document the original location of the victim or objects that you observe being moved.

g. Consider search and seizure items to determine the necessity of obtaining consent to search/and or obtaining a search warrant.

*Note:* persons should not smoke, chew tobacco, use the telephone or bathroom, eat or drink, move any items including weapons (unless necessary for the safety and well being of persons at the scene), adjust the thermostat or open windows or doors (maintain scene as found), touch anything unnecessarily (note and document any items moved), reposition moved items, litter, or spit within the established boundaries of the scene.

*Summary:* Establishing boundaries is a critical aspect in controlling the integrity of evidentiary material.

## Turn Over Control of the Scene and Brief Investigator(s) in Charge

*Principal:* Briefing the investigator(s) taking charge assists in controlling the crime scene and helps establish further investigative responsibilities.

*Policy:* The initial responding officer(s) at the scene shall provide a detailed crime scene briefing to the investigator(s) in charge at the scene.

*Procedure:* The initial responding officer(s) should:

a.   Brief the investigator(s) taking charge

b.   Assist in controlling the scene

c.   Turn over responsibility for the documentation of entry/exit

d.   Remain at the scene until relieved of duty.

*Summary:* The scene briefing is the only opportunity for the next in command to obtain initial aspects of the crime scene prior to subsequent investigation.

## Document Actions and Observations

*Principal:* All activities conducted and observations made at the crime scene must be documented as soon as possible after the event to preserve information.

*Policy:* Documentation must be maintained as a permanent record.

*Procedure:* The initial responding officer(s) should document:

a.   Observations of the crime scene, including the location of persons and items within the crime scene and the appearance and condition upon arrival.

b.   Conditions upon arrival (e.g., lights on/off; shades up/down, open/ closed; doors, windows, open/closed; smells; ice, liquids; movable furniture; weather; temperature; and personal items)

c.   Personnel information from witnesses, victims, suspects, and any statements comments made.

d.   Own actions and actions of others.

*Summary:* The initial responding officer(s) at the crime scene must produce clear, concise, documented information encompassing his or her observations and actions. This documentation is vital in providing information to substantiate investigative considerations.

## Contamination Control

*Principal:* Contamination control and preventing cross contamination at single multiple scenes is essential to maintaining the safety of personnel and the integrity of evidence.

*Policy:* The investigator(s) in charge shall require all personnel to follow procedures to ensure scene safety and evidence integrity.

*Procedure:* Other responders and/or team members shall:

    a.   Limit scene access to people directly involved in scene processing.

    b.   Follow established entry/exit routes at the scene

    c.   Identify first responders and consider collection of elimination samples.

    d.   Designate secure area for trash and equipment.

    e.   Use personnel protective equipment (PPE) to prevent contamination of personnel and to minimize scene contamination

    f.   Clean/sanitize or dispose of tools/equipment and personnel protective equipment between evidence collections and or scenes.

    g.   Utilize single-use equipment when performing direct collection of biological specimens.

*Summary:* Minimize contamination by being safe, clean, and careful to ensure the welfare of personnel and the integrity of the evidence.

## Documentation

*Principal:* An assessment of the scene determines what kind of documentation is needed (e.g., photography, video, sketches, measurements, notes).

*Policy:* The investigator(s) in charge shall ensure documentation of the scene.

*Procedure:* the team member(s) should:

    a.   Review assessment of the scene to determine the type of documentation needed.

    b.   Coordinate photographs, video, sketches, measurements, and notes.

    c.   Photograph:

        • Scene utilizing overall, medium, and close up coverage.

        • Evidence to be collected with and without measurements scale and or evidence identifiers.

- Victims, suspects, witnesses, crowd, and vehicles.
- Additional perspectives (e.g., aerial photographs, witness' view, area under body once body is removed).

d.  Videotape as optional supplement to photos.

e.  Prepare preliminary sketch (es) and measure.

- Immediate area of the scene, noting case identifiers and indicating north on the sketch.
- Relative location of items of evidence and correlate evidence items with evidence records.
- Evidence prior to movement.
- Rooms, furniture or other objects.
- Distance to adjacent buildings or other landmarks.

f.  Generate notes at the scene:

- Documenting location of the scene, time of arrival, and time of departure.
- Describing the scene as it appears.
- Recording transient evidence (e.g., smells, sounds, sights, and conditions (e.g., temperature, weather).
- Documenting circumstances that require departures from usual procedures.

*Summary:* A well-documented scene ensures the integrity of the investigation and provides a permanent record for later evaluation.

## Collect, Preserve, Inventory, Package, Transport, and Submit Evidence

*Principal:* The handling of physical evidence is one of the most important factors of their investigation.

*Policy:* The team members shall ensure the effective collection, preservation, packaging, and transport of evidence.

***Procedure:*** The team member(s) should:

a.   Maintain scene security throughout processing and until the scene is released.

b.   Document the collection of evidence by recording its location at the scene, date of collection, and who collects it.

c.   Collect each item identified as evidence.

d.   Establish the chain of custody.

e.   Obtain standard/reference samples from the scene.

f.   Obtain control samples

g.   Consider obtaining elimination samples.

h.   Immediately secure electronically recorded evidence (e.g., answering machine tapes, surveillance camera videotapes, computers) from the vicinity.

i.   Identify and secure evidence in containers (e.g. label, date, initial, container) at the crime scene. Different types of evidence require different containers (e.g. porous, nonporous, crushproof).

j.   Package items to avoid contamination and cross contamination.

k.   Document the condition of firearms/weapons prior to rendering them safe for transportation and submission.

l.   Avoid excessive handling of evidence after its collected.

m.   Maintain evidence at the scene in a manner designed to diminish degradation or loss.

n.   Transport and submit evidence items for secure storage.

***Summary:*** Evidence at crime scenes that is in the process of documentation, collection, preservation, or packaging should be handled with attention to scene integrity and protection from contamination or deleterious change. During the processing of the scene, and following documentation, evidence should be appropriately packaged, labeled and maintained in a secure temporary manner until final packaging and submission to a secured evidence storage facility or the crime laboratory.

The above recommendations were made by a group named "The Technical Working Group on Crime Scene Investigation." The group included members from the defense bar as well as law enforcement personnel from more than 35 states. The aforementioned recommendations came in a simple 48-page publication. It is an excellent reference tool for what should happen at crime scenes.

We enthusiastically endorse their recommendations. If all crime scenes were worked as the group recommended, we are certain that the wrongful conviction rate would be greatly reduced from its current out-of-control status. As we have seldom, if ever, seen a crime scene processed utilizing all of these recommendations, we are not hopeful that these recommendations and standards are uniformly utilized.

As a consequence we would encourage you to always pay close attention as to how your crime scene was processed. In addition, we would encourage defense personnel to hold all law enforcement agencies to these simple standards. Whenever you find yourself with a wrongful conviction case, the preceding standards will hopefully assist you in determining what was or was not accomplished.

### Preparing for your visit to the old crime scene

When you are sitting around sucking on those lattes, you have to figure out what you want to accomplish at the crime scene. We would recommend a minimum of three visits. The first visit to the crime scene should accomplish the following:

- Tape measure and sketch scene
- Photograph scene form all angles and from where witnesses previously stated they were standing
- Try and visit scene as close to the exact day and time of the reported incident. In other words, if the crime occurred on June 2nd at 8:40 p.m., you want to be out there at least one time at that date and hour so you can recapture the true feeling of what it may have been like when the crime occurred.
- Videotape the scene to help memorialize what you see at the time of examination.

After you have had an opportunity to visit an old crime scene you will start to get a feeling for what could have happened, and consequently what could have been reported wrong initially. The second step is for you and your team to carefully evaluate the crime scene paperwork and determine what, if anything is missing from it.

As we have previously indicated the importance of gathering the complete file, we won't restate the obvious. However, if there is a place that does have missing records this will be it. As with the rest of the case, missing files or pages will wreak havoc with your case. The problem is that this paperwork is routinely overlooked for a myriad of reasons, the best being is that it is usually pretty boring stuff. Because it's boring it's not really sexy, so it has a habit of falling through the cracks.

In addition to locating all of the crime scene records it is important to reexamine any transcripts or portions thereof which focus on or talk about the crime scene. This is especially critical when any eyewitnesses are talking about or testifying about what they have seen or not seen. On many occasions we have been able to prove conclusively that a particular witness was lying about what they saw or didn't see based on what we have observed at the crime scene. This also comes in very handy when you are interviewing old witnesses. Often this is when police misconduct issues start peeking out from under the covers.

## Your Second Visit

You have accomplished your initial crime scene visit and you now have gathered all kinds of interesting data and information that can be checked against the initial police **generated** reports. This visit is always a good time to drag counsel out of the courthouse or gin mill and have him or her see the scene for themselves. We are always amazed when attorneys who are responsible for examining witnesses have never been to the crime scene. Without counsel having a direct knowledge about the crime scene, witnesses are free to get away with creating facts and lying about others. *This is where witnesses are creating and lying and getting away with it.*

*This is due to counsel having a lack of direct knowledge about the crime scene.* It is and should be a routine that young litigators have established early in their careers. If not, how could counsel ever file a motion *for a jury view with the court?*

## Maps

Always make an effort to obtain detailed maps of the area. *In addition to your own photos and those that law enforcement authored.* We would recommend that aerial photographs be obtained. These aerial photos should reflect how the crime scene looked at the time of the incident and how it looks now. These maps and photos are critical when it comes to demonstrative evidence and jurisdictional issues.

## The Third Visit

You have hopefully at this point obtained an excellent feel for your crime scene. You have verified or disproved some facts, and you now have to devote some serious thought to what else you need to accomplish. This is when you want to start canvassing the area for witnesses who were not found initially or were purposely concealed from the defense. It does not matter how long a period of time has elapsed. There is always somebody around who can help.

This visit is also an opportunity to bring back witnesses who are cooperating with your investigation. These witnesses are invaluable in helping determine what was missed initially or purposely withheld from the defense. Witnesses, businesses and neighbors move or die. Life circumstances change quickly. All of these problems contribute to making your life difficult. Nevertheless, the effort is worth it.

## Physical Evidence

At some point in your investigation you will need to inspect the evidence that the responsible agency gathered and stored. Some of this evidence will have made it to the courthouse. Most of it will be either in the possession of the police or the prosecutor's office. Do not ever forfeit the opportunity to review physical evidence.

When examining the physical evidence make sure there are two of you present. One has to document what was viewed and the other has to inspect it. Always verify everything that has been inventoried. If something was destroyed there should be a court order authorizing its destruction. If not, be very leery.

Verify that the evidence is being properly stored and secured. Look at chain of custody forms and note who has been signing out and moving evidence around. Any names that are not familiar to you already should be checked closely. Multiple sign-outs by the same person is a red flag. You will have to verify why the evidence was being fooled with.

## Summary & Conclusions

The crime scene workup in any given wrongful conviction case is always important. It may wind up being one of your main themes or arguments for innocence. It can often dispel facts from fantasy. Our good fortune in these matters has been incredible. It was not an accident that we discovered these problems with the states' case. It happens because of painful attention to detail. The efforts put forth in closely examining this area of investigation are well worth the time.

# 6

## *Interviews & Interrogations Conducting Them & Overcoming Them*

"To doubt everything or to believe anything are two equally convenient solutions; both dispense with the necessity of reflection."

*—Jules Henri Poincare, 1913*

There is no one single bigger issue to overcome then a confession made by your client in the case against him or her. More specifically, your client's mouth will almost certainly help launch him into the bowels of the penitentiary. The ability to keep one's mouth shut is a rare talent. Consequently, this is almost always a burning issue in every wrongful conviction case. Conversely, if you do not have the ability to interview people of interest in any given case, you will not be doing this work long. So, if you don't read anything else in this book, at least read this chapter.

Interviews differ very much from interrogations in that an interview is always an attempt to gather information and an interrogation is always a confrontation. When interviews occur you are always seeking information. When an interrogation happens you are almost always verifying information you already possess. Any interview can quickly turn into an interrogation. When that happens to your client it is always a bad sign.

If you are going to be conducting interviews in any given case, there are a number of things you must do before you jump into your Jag and go about town talking to folks. With few exceptions you should always learn as much as you can about any subject with whom you are contemplating an interview. Grabbing a name and an address and flying out the door to interview someone is not professional.

As we are talking about witnesses in a wrongful conviction case there will normally be a host of information on this individual. In most wrongful conviction cases, both the government and defense team will have interviewed the witness. Consequently, there may be trial transcripts, depositions, police reports and defense reports on the target individual.

All of these reports should be thoroughly reviewed prior to any contact with this witness. An up-to-date background investigation should also be done. Remember, intelligence is sometimes more important then what the witness will actually say. Witnesses often lie or embellish when being interviewed. I know you're thinking, "That never happens to me," but when it does you need to be prepared so that you know you are being lied to or conned. Much of what you will be inquiring about will be in these documents, so you can never be too prepared.

When conducting the pre-interview background investigation, we would suggest that you start with the following:

- Civil Court Indexes (from every jurisdiction that the subject has lived in)
- Criminal court records (From every previous area subject has resided in)
- Voter's registration
- Corporate records
- Bankruptcy Filings
- Motor Vehicle records
- Assessor records
- Traffic records
- Real estate transfers
- Databases
- Proprietary data
- Internet Inquiries
- News media
- Business data

If you were in the position of having subpoena power the next level of information that you should seek would include the following:

- Banking records
- Police reports (when not available through FOI request)
- Medical records
- Telephone records
- Psychological or Psychiatric Reports
- School records and transcripts
- Credit Reports
- Employment Records
- Medical Insurance records
- Income tax returns
- Credit card details
- Pre-sentence investigation reports
- Plea bargain deals in any case
- Victim Assistance grants or financial assistance
- Prison records to include diplomacy and intelligence records
- Previous mug shots

As you can see, your inquiries are only limited by your imagination. Anyone over the age of twenty has a history. Your job is to find it. The above suggestive areas of inquiry are only a starting point. All too often interviews are conducted without the benefit of having done a complete background check. Sometimes it is unavoidable. However, when you are not armed with as much information as possible, you are giving up any advantage that you may have had.

After having back grounded a witness, and having familiarized yourself with what the historical records, you are now ready to approach the witness. The following is the most crucial step in the investigation. If a witness refuses to speak with you all of your efforts will be greatly diminished.

We cannot stress this point enough. Over the years volumes have been written about interviewing witnesses. Very little attention has been paid to how one gets a witness to cooperate. Lawyers seem to think that all one has to do is sprinkle a little fairy dust on a potential witness and they will truthfully and honestly have a frank discussion with the investigator. We wish that it were that easy. The truth of the matter is those witnesses, in every case, almost never have a good reason to speak with you. If a witness had time to honestly assess his or her reason for cooperating with a defense investigator, they would no doubt come to the conclusion "that there ain't no percentage in it for me."

Add on the fact that the police, the prosecutors, their mother, spouse, significant other, etc., will almost always advise then against doing an interview, and you now have a problem. This is why we do not ever recommend that anyone other then a true professional ever attempt the initial contact with any witness. All too often any chance of interviewing either a friendly or potentially hostile witness is lost forever when the initial approach is made in anything less then a well thought-out strategy.

To call or not to call, that is the question. Except with well-known, friendly, cooperative witnesses we recommend that no advance warning is given. Don't call, write or fax. Simply show up on the witnesses' doorstep and start. The minute that most witnesses have any type of warning that you are seeking them out, nothing but bad things will happen. Police and prosecutors are contacted. Lawyers are called. Advice is sought. Plans are developed. In other words, instead of having a lone witness to contend with you are now dealing with a platoon of commandos whose sole mission will be to thwart the interview. This may seem like simple common sense advice, but after having been burned by hundreds of incidents like the foregoing, this advice must be repeated and repeated often.

Although this is not by any means a basic text, as with any sport, the basics are what carry you through to the more difficult aspects of any single case. With that in mind, how you dress, how you present yourself, and what you initially say and do mean everything. I mention these things with the advantage of mature reflection, something one cannot attain without many years of experience. Anyone can be the Monday morning quarterback. We realize the intricacies of conducting a successful interview. We know that if it were easy, there would be no need for this or any other instructive type text. Having said that, it is still worth repeating.

### *Ghetto 101*

People are generally products of their environment. If you were raised in an affluent upper-class area, your life experiences will reflect that. Similarly, if you were raised in abject poverty in the inner city, your experiences and sense of self will reflect those circumstances. No matter where you were raised or schooled, what is important, no, critical, is your ability to adapt to whatever environment you find yourself in. Failure to do so will result in getting yourself killed, badly injured or worse yet; having it happen to someone you are training or mentoring.

For several years I have been teaching a class to journalism students at Northwestern University in Chicago. We call a portion of the class Ghetto 101. Before your sensitive side emerges and you start thinking this is a racist or politically incorrect title. Relax. We could easily call it: Trailer Park 101, Hillbilly Heaven 101, Meth Freak 101 or Skinhead 101. Ghetto 101 works and we have stuck with it. It is politically incorrect, but we're in the business of saving lives, not pleasing sensitive people. The title is unimportant. What we teach can save your life. That is important. What we attempt to convey and what we have conveyed, very successfully thus far, is survival.

At the end of the day all we want to do is come back home in one piece. Everything else is insignificant. Getting the interview. Impressing your peers. If you fail to get home in one piece you have failed. If you manage to get a young student or intern injured you have really failed. You have not only jeopardized somebody's future and career, you have potentially put an entire innocence project at risk. If you can stop thinking about all of the movie and book deals for a few seconds and think about what is really critical, you and those around you should come out of this no worse for the wear and tear.

If you are the murder police (homicide detectives) you have a distinct advantage when you are conducting interviews and interrogations. You have your office and the unbridled power of the state behind you. The murder police control all aspects of this part of the investigation and are at a huge advantage as to what they can do and how they can do it. You, on the other hand, enjoy none of those benefits. What those of you who have been doing this for more then a little while have is your wits and the ability to think on your feet. That's it. If you feel that all of this is easy and that your natural, superior intelligence will help you fake it until you make it, you are dead wrong.

The first part of Ghetto 101 is the dress code. For the sake of clarity we classify the ghetto as a high-crime rate, poor socio-economic area where you would not go on vacation. It has nothing to do with race and everything to do with economics.

What is of little consequence is the race of its inhabitants. It is always a potentially very dangerous place. It's dangerous for its residents and really dangerous for those of you who do not live or work there. In the ghetto there is an abundance of guns, dope and alcohol. This mixture is an explosive recipe. There is no good time to visit there. There are only better times then others.

Our preference for timing is to go very early in the morning, or after its gotten dark out. The reasons for this are fairly straightforward. In the morning when people are just beginning to stir, they are not on top of their game. They are groggy, they haven't had a lot of time to mentally wake up and they are just not prepared to deal with this intrusion. In other words, they will generally respond in a manner that is advantageous to you.

These early a.m. visits also work well when you are attempting to interview people who generally have a lot of distractions present such as spouses, children etc. The least amount of people at the party, the less chance of interference and coaching. Unlike the murder police you are conducting an interview on their turf, not yours.

### Preparing for the Interview

You have to try and gain every advantage you can. As with every aspect of a wrongful conviction investigation, nothing is easy. You have to work for every break you can get. Nothing comes gift wrapped.

Prior to arriving at your destination a pre-interview meeting should be held. At this meeting is the person who is conducting the interview, anyone who will be assisting them or accompanying him or her and the case guru (the person who is really familiar with all aspects of the case). The attorney should be there if they are involved at this juncture.

At this meeting all technical and equipment requirements should be discussed thoroughly. The following equipment and their purpose are explained below.

- Legal pads and plenty of working pens. You can never have enough paper and pens.

- Miniature audiocassette recorder and blank tapes. In the event that you need to record a statement or make verbal notes, this is a must. Always make sure that you test the batteries and have plenty of extra or an alternative power supply.

- Video camera with at least five blank tapes. Once again make sure you have plenty of batteries.

- Camera tripod for camera and video camera

- A good working five or six cell metal flashlight that works and is heavy. They make excellent door knockers and personal protection devices

- Pepper spray for those frisky 120 pound Rottweilers and pitbulls. The flashlight will only work if Fido is gnawing on your partner.

- A working cell phone

The above is the minimum amount of props and necessities that should be considered. Having a working vehicle with a full tank of gas, change for pay phones, and enough money to buy a witness lunch is also advisable. While on this subject of money you should be prepared for the witness who wishes to be paid for his or her time. Don't do it. Explain to them how much trouble you could both get into for doing that. Remember informants and snitches are paid. Witnesses are not.

For example it is acceptable to take a witness to a fast food restaurant or diner for a burger and fries. It's not OK to take them down to the local tavern and buy them eight or nine beers. If it feels inappropriate it generally is inappropriate. Remember at some point all of your actions will be closely examined by the state. If you do <u>anything</u> that could be considered illegal, unethical or immoral they will hold you accountable. You do not want to become the lightning rod of the case in this manner.

The clothes make the man or woman, right? Indeed they do. The trick of course is not to dress like your favorite rock star, but to fit in the environment in which you're working. Dressing the part is a critical component of the interview. Your age and background will determine in part as to how you will dress. Middle-aged white guys should not attempt to dress in the latest urban hip-hop wear. Dress your age but don't over do it.

If you are interviewing or canvassing in a high-crime area, the first rule is dress defensively. Wear clothes that you can move in. Tennis shoes or sneakers are appropriate. When that 80 pound German Shepard rounds the corner, you had better be able to move fast. The Bruno Magli shoes should be left at home. Casual dress is encouraged, but not so casual as to not be taken seriously.

When your interview is taking place in a more affluent area it may be time to drag out the suit and tie or business attire. The goal is to gain a certain amount of respect with the person you are interviewing. You do not want them to have a first impression that has them thinking you are trying to imitate Britney Spears. Save the belly and muscle shirts for the company picnic. This is not a fashion show, it's an interview.

### *Gaining Entrance*

You have prepared, planned and dressed appropriately. You are now on the witness's front porch, you and your prover are waiting, Mr. Perjury is coming to the door and he is not happy. His mortgage is late, his wife has filed for divorce and his teenager is in rehab. In short, you are the last person he wants to see. He is cranky, pissed and does not want to talk about something that happened ten years ago. All he wants at this moment is for the two of you to disappear. If he were Captain Kirk, the two of you would be disappearing.

He opens the door a crack and says, "What do you two assholes want?" You now have exactly ten to thirty seconds to convince Mr. Perjury to talk to you. If you don't, he is slamming the door shut and your client is never getting out of jail.

Do you think this is made up? A fairy tale? No, it is absolutely a true story. The six months you have spent reviewing the case. The five hundred dollars you spent in database searches to find Mr. Perjury. Your client's eventual release and freedom. It's all gone if you don't convince Mr. Perjury to speak with you, right now. All of this is flowing through your system so quickly you are in a state of shock. How do you do it? How are you going to pull this one off?

I have just written over 2,700 words getting you to this point. Do you think it's still easy? If you do, you've never done this for a living. Because this is where you earn your keep. This is what you do, and you have to do it now. There is no tomorrow, no second chance. Mr. Perjury better be giving you a statement forthwith or you better be on the phone with your travel agent.

Let's first examine what *you don't do.* You don't threaten Mr. Perjury. You don't claim to be a police officer or representative of the state. You don't yell. You don't panic. Most importantly, you don't show any fear. If you do, Mr. Perjury will smell it and he will beam you off the front porch at warp speed like Captain Kirk or Spock would.

What you do is remain calm and start talking. You talk and Mr. Perjury listens. You do not let him talk, not yet. You talk until Mr. Perjury relaxes, or invites you in. If you have to, you sit on that front porch and you talk for three hours if that is what it's going to take. You remain polite, deferential, but firm. You are at his house asking him for something. He didn't knock on your door at 7:30 in the morning.

What you tell Mr. Perjury, over and over again, is that you only need a few minutes of his time. You have to convince Mr. Perjury that talking to you is in his best interest, not yours. You tell him that if he doesn't want ten more visits from other interested parties, he will talk to you now. You explain to him how a platoon of evil, good for nothing lawyers are preparing reams of subpoenas just for him. You tell him you are here to make his life easy and less complicated. You tell him it will only take a few minutes. When you've been there for two hours and he starts getting really agitated, you still tell him, "only a couple of more minutes."

Now, guys like Mr. Perjury are tough guys. They have survived wars, divorces, jail, the police, bankruptcy and ill tempered wives and girlfriends, concurrently. You are not even in the same league as the rest of his life issues. But, what Mr. Perjury doesn't know is that you already know all of this. You have pulled his criminal record. You have found the summons and complaint from his girlfriend for paternity testing. You know his wife had him served with the documents. You know when he filed bankruptcy two years ago he had assets of eighteen dollars. You know all this because you did your homework. Now the trick is how you use it to facilitate an interview.

## *Fact Gathering*

The first rule of getting Mr. Perjury to cooperate is sympathy. You have to convince Mr. Perjury that you are just like him. It doesn't matter that's its not true, he has to believe it, you don't. He has got to feel comfortable. He has to think, "This is not such a bad person, maybe a pain in my ass, but hell, I'll give him or her five minutes."

Some of the more frequent excuses we have heard from witnesses who are reluctant to speak with us are:

- *I'm busy come back next week*
- *I'm cooking breakfast and the pancakes are burning*
- *I don't want to be involved*
- *The police/prosecutor said you people are the devil and I shouldn't talk to you*
- *I'm having sex with my boyfriend come back in ten minutes*
- *We're getting high right now, come back tomorrow*
- *Your client is a piece of shit and I'm glad he's getting juiced next week*
- *I will shoot your dog ass if you don't get off my property right now*
- *I'm not really the person you should be talking to about this to*
- *I have to supervise the maid now, call my attorney he'll talk to you*
- *My Minister told me not to help your client*
- *The police told me that their gang is bigger and meaner then your client's gang*
- *What you'll give me if I talk to you (pick one; money, dope, sex)*

These are the usual set of excuses that witnesses give in trying to avoid you. The witness will go to any length to avoid being involved. Some of their reasons are valid. We would never want to intentionally disturb the maid's routine or interrupt a good high. However, your chance of succeeding later rather then now is almost nonexistent.

Instead of thinking about how Starbucks just burned you for eight bucks for that triple Espresso Frappuccino, you had better be concentrating on how to overcome the witness's lame excuses.

This is a good time to make some helpful suggestions that may help you avoid some problems later. The first suggestion is to remind you that although you may have once been a local police officer, state's attorney investigator, FBI agent, etc., you are now just a citizen. As such you no longer enjoy the privileges you once enjoyed.

You cannot display badges, weapons, radios and the other trappings of office. You cannot call the SWAT team if things get out of control. You cannot threaten a witness with jail, grand juries, and perjury charges. In your old life things were different, very different. You could bring down the wrath of God. You could drag them out of the house in handcuffs. You could subject them to endless grand jury appearances. Life was good, it was fair, and you were north of evil.

Well that's too bad. You are now just an ordinary private investigator. You may be licensed, but that license is fairly worthless. It has no power, no clout, nothing. For all practical purposes you have about as much power as the 7-11 clerk down on the corner. All you really have is your charm and positive attitude. If you're having a bad day, week or month, suppress it. You have to be on, and you have to be focused. If you're not, the interview, if you get it, will probably go poorly.

Now, while you are making your new friend, what is the prover you brought along for this fine educational experience doing? Well, he or she had better be watching what's going on, or the two of you may become police report subjects listed as deceased. Rule number one. The prover is always watching Mr. Perjury's hands. Mr. Perjury is not going to shoot or stab you with his feet or mouth. If something bad is going to happen it will come from his hands. The prover is going to be looking for Mr. Perjury's friends and colleagues. He or she is the safety valve.

The prover is there to witness a statement and make sure that the two of you don't become statistics and minor newspaper stories. The prover once in the house is going to be looking for problems. The following is always a problem and should be taken very seriously:

- Any weapons in open view. i.e., guns, knives, rifles, shotguns, cross bows, martial arts equipment, etc.

- Any signs of drugs or drug paraphernalia

- Large pets that bite

- Other adults in the house who don't appear to live there
- Children who are inappropriately dressed or cared for

In short anything that can be a danger to you or is very suspicious in nature. Remember, you don't know what you're walking in on. Mr. Perjury and his armed robbery crew may have been cutting up the booty from last night when you arrived. He may have a drug deal being prepared in the kitchen. He might have his 15-year-old niece naked in the bedroom. The point is you may be walking into an unknown, highly dangerous situation that has nothing to do with you or your case. Always remember that when your little play was cast in hell, there were no angels around. We would suggest that this is not a good time after all for this interview. Always be conscious of your surroundings.

### *Safety Issues*

Although we just spent the last several pages telling you why you must interview Mr. Perjury, never let the interview interfere with your continued breathing. There is always another day. While were on the subject of safety, let's examine your taste in accessories.

To go to the interview armed with a weapon or not is a personal decision based on a number of factors. The short answer is yes. Whenever possible go armed and prepared for a worst case scenario. This of course is only true if you have the proper licenses and permits. If you are not properly licensed you are in all likelihood committing a felony. Remember you do not want to be the subject of any police report. Now we realize that some private investigators really like their accessories. They love guns and handcuffs and mace and all of those really macho cool things.

Here we go again. These toys may be really cool and really impressive to some people, but to our modest way of thinking they are like bikini underwear. Very sexy, but best left hidden and put away. In other words if you are sporting the latest in nickel-plated, semi-automatic handguns, keep it with your bikini: Under something and totally hidden from the public and the individual you are attempting to interview. A weapon or personal protection device should never be displayed, not under any circumstances. Not unless you are getting ready to use it for real.

If you haven't figured it out yet, let us give you a mild example on about how these accessories can ruin the day. You have gotten Mr. Perjury to give you a great statement on videotape. The statement is everything you hoped for. He tells you about how he was threatened and coerced by the police. He tells you that his previous statements and testimony were a total fabrication. He tells you that he has found God, and that he is coming clean now because his conscience is bothering him. In short, he has just really wrecked the states case in chief.

Now, fast forward six months. You have turned over your video per local discovery rules. The DA and his investigators are watching this tape and they are not happy. It makes them look incompetent, corrupt, etc. The DA is hotter than the sidewalk in Miami in August. He tells his star investigators to get out to Mr. Perjury's house and get this misunderstanding straightened out before the TV stations pick up on it. He tells them that all of their careers are in jeopardy if Mr. Perjury sticks to his current story. In short, he tells them that they had better call their travel agents if they don't get this straightened out.

The boys hop in their unmarked squad car and drive out to Mr. Perjury's home where they find him sitting on the front porch with his posse. The boys, who are not in any mood for Mr. Perjury's charming personality or wit, decide to take the direct approach with Mr. Perjury. They tell him that they are in possession of your video starring him. They tell him that they are sure that Mr. Perjury would not have done something so stupid as to embarrass them and their boss, the DA. Mr. Perjury, who is in the middle of a great buzz, tells the boys that he really doesn't "give two shits about their problem." Furthermore, they can get back in their police car and get off of his private property.

The boys as you can imagine are not pleased with this response. They promptly throw Mr. Perjury to the ground, handcuff him at gunpoint and take him back to police headquarters as an uncooperative material witness. The long ride back to the police station has a sobering effect on Mr. Perjury. He quickly decides that he is far more worried about these two detectives and the DA then he is you. He assesses his options, considers the pros and cons and quickly decides that you hoodwinked him. Furthermore, he tells the detectives that while you were interviewing him, you kept displaying your nickel-plated 9mm. He indicates that if he hadn't felt threatened he would have never told all of those lies about the boys and that nice DA feller.

You have, by showing off your accessories, unnecessarily complicated your life beyond words. Your statement is ruined. Perjury is written off as a witness who will say anything to please anybody. The DA is considering charging you with witness tampering. The media is calling you "a cop wannabe." Was displaying your accessories for vanity or macho reasons worth it? We think not.

The forgoing was just a minor example of just how perilous this interviewing of witnesses can be. You must always think about what you do and how you do it. You must take every potential problem under consideration and have a contingency plan to deal with it. The damage that you may cause for a seemingly minor act can be devastating to your client. Always proceed with extreme caution.

### *The Interview*

It is very difficult to set any hard and fast rules for any one single interview. All interviews are different. The chances that identical circumstances will occur the same way in every interview are slim. There is a different twist to every interview.

With that in mind, there are also a lot of similar activities that you should be watching for. These are without exception something you should practice:

- Always observe the witness's physical appearance: Is the witness clean and well groomed? Is the witness sober? Well spoken? Well educated? Is he or she nervous or upset?

- Body language: A critical component of any interview. Is the witness hostile? Overly friendly? Are they sitting down and talking in a normal tone of voice? Are they overly or suspiciously emotional? Do they maintain adequate eye contact? Are their arms folded or relaxed? Are their legs continually crossed? Are they answering questions with more questions? Are they smoking excessively? Are they attempting to buy time with delaying tactics? Is there an unusual pause between answers, even simple ones?

- Observe hand and body movements: is the witness picking at lint constantly? Playing with their jewelry? Hiding their hands between their legs? Adjusting or cleaning glasses?

If you are observing these types of behaviors by a witness, you are probably being lied to. Your job at this point is not to confront, but just observe. This is all ammunition for when you get down to the tough questions. It is a preview of what is going to happen later.

Assuming that you have gained the cooperation of the witness and they have something of substance to offer, you now have to decide how you are going to memorialize their statement. This is also an area that you have to ease into. Setting up a camera and turning it on will not do. You have to ease into just how you are going to document this statement. There are really four accepted ways, they are:

1. If the witness is reluctant and will not sign anything, then you have to audiotape record the statement. Make sure that you identify any third parties present.

2. If the witness will sign a written statement, then you write up the statement yourself. Never let a witness write his or her own statement. Write the statement in affidavit form. Have the witness initial each page and every crosscut or misspelled word. At a later date send a copy of the statement to the witness.

3. Take an official court reported statement from the witness. If the witness is old, ill or willing, get a court reporter to take his or her statement. This statement when done right is a very powerful and credible statement.

4. Last but hardly least, is the videotaped statement. This is the author's personal favorite for any number of reasons. Most Americans love television. TV raised them. Anything that they see and hear has a longer lasting impression. Witnesses are seen as they were at the time the statement was made. Videotape clearly shows that the statement was made freely and voluntarily. If a court reporter is available to take down the interview in conjunction with the videotaping, so much the better.

### *Caveats*

We would caution all but the most experienced investigator when it comes to audio or video generated statements. Witnesses have a habit of blurting out anything during these sessions. It takes years of experience to control the give and take of an interview. You do not want Mr. Perjury saying something that will destroy your case in three seconds. Do not do this unless you are sure you can control the question and answer portion of the interview.

There are a number of issues that have to be covered during the interview or statement portion. In the very beginning you must identify whom you are working for and just what your position is. Do not assume that whoever is reviewing this at a later date, will know who you are. This also clarifies the "You identified yourself as a police officer, detective, FBI agent etc, didn't you" question. It is one less thing that you will be picked on for at a later date.

Always have the witness state their own name and other identifying data. Always have the witness acknowledge that he or she is making this statement voluntarily. Always have the witness acknowledge on the record that they haven't been bribed, promised anything or otherwise coerced.

## *The Interrogation*

Interrogation is not high tea at the Drake Hotel. It is not a pleasant little chat between two friends. It is a highly-charged emotional event where you are accusing a witness or subject of an investigation of lying about or participating in some kind of illegal activity. Interrogation is very much like pornography, difficult to describe, but when you see it you'll recognize it. Interrogation is not for the shy or faint of heart. It is complicated and dirty. Not everyone is meant to be an interrogator. If you are taking this role on in the wrongful conviction investigation you had better be well trained and had a lot of experience.

Brains, not brawn, will be your biggest asset in an interrogation. You have to have a plan and you have to stick with it. It is not a team sport. Only one person should conduct the interrogation. Two should always witness any admissions or confessions. Literally volumes have been published on this subject. There are half a dozen excellent schools of instruction run by both the government and private industry. We would strongly recommend that if you haven't attended one, you do so. The rules and nuances are not something that can be taught here. We can only give you the down and dirty version of it.

The first area of consideration in the proposed interrogation of any witness is location. Once again you are not the murder police so it's not likely that you will be taking anybody anywhere. In all likelihood you may be doing your interrogation at a fast food restaurant, a car, or someone's living room.

The key under those circumstances is to get as much privacy as possible. Keep all distractions to a minimum. Turn off those all important cell phones and pagers. You have to be at the height of your persuasive powers and the witness has to be able to pay attention.

When an interview turns into an interrogation you will know it. At least you'd better know it at that point. Most of the time when an interrogation is going to take place, you have planned it. You know what you are going to say, how you are going to say it, and what your plan is going to be to get the subject to confess to something or change the substance of a previously made statement.

We are going to now go way out on the limb with our brethren in the defense bar. They for the most part have a strong dislike and mistrust of any confession. They especially dislike confessions that are gotten with guile, tricks or methods. They are especially distrustful of the most widely used method called the Reid method. I have seen and heard them call the Reid method "psychological torture." Ouch.

The author has been extensively trained by the folks at John Reid and Associates and respectfully disagrees. Like any well known and successful method, it can and has been abused. It can be manipulated and abused by anyone who has a basic understanding of it.

We would tell you that when we have successfully used the Reid method in obtaining confessions that have set innocent men free from death row, the carping and complaining were nonexistent. We would also tell you that in Reid's textbook the second chapter is titled "Initial Precautionary Measures for the Protection of the Innocent" Reid and associates methods are the most widely taught method in the world. They are the masters of interviews and interrogations. If you haven't had formal training in this area, these are the folks to get it from. Although abuse of their method does happen, when properly employed it is the most successful method in the discipline.

Flipping a witness or getting a subject to confess to a crime is the result of you the interviewer exercising patience, persistence and knowledge about your subject and witness. If the subject suspects (even on a subconscious level) that you are impatient or hurried they will almost never come around to the truth. They will delay, lie, create and stall for as long as necessary. This is a battle of wits and patience, not brute strength.

Telling lies or using trickery and deceit on a subject during the course of an interrogation is acceptable, legal, and ethical. They have to be well placed lies and they have to be believable based on the facts that you have developed. The subject doesn't necessarily have to believe them, but he must be unsure of their validity and veracity. The legality of these methods is well established. Judges and juries will not generally punish you for telling a lie to a witness. They will punish you for lying to them. When you lie to a witness, be careful and judicious.

### Dealing with False Statements
### Undoing the Damage

We have all heard attorneys say that they really don't know if their client committed the crime or not. They go on to say that it generally doesn't matter to them, that they have a job to do regardless of their client's involvement. Well, that may be OK for theatrics or legal ethics courses, but for a practical matter we think you better have a real clue as to your client's involvement in any given case. Resources are always scarce so you had better learn to save time and money and dispense with the fairy tales, and "I wish" scenarios.

The first stop in most cases is the local jail for a "come-to-Jesus meeting" with our client. For the more affluent ones who are out on bond we can meet anywhere that provides privacy. As with most things in life it is not necessarily the message itself, but how the message is delivered that determines what is received. You must patiently and painstakingly explain to your client the boundaries of privileged communication. They must be comfortable with the premise. This is often easier said then done, but you have to get that message through.

The client has to be made to understand that his recourses are: a) not unlimited b) that your time is valuable, and c) that wasting time on any lies that he generates will only hurt him or her later. As with most clients they have to realize that lying to you is extremely counter productive and will only damage their already perilous legal position.

As we are primarily concerned with wrongful conviction cases here, we will assume that the client has been telling the truth about his innocence and that all of the above is unnecessary. However, it does merit repeating under the guise of protecting yourself and saving ungodly amounts of energy and time on entertaining fairy tales that the client has told more gullible individuals than you.

When we were young investigators, we were deeply saddened to hear that the prosecutor had our client on tape or video admitting his or her involvement in a crime. We were also shell shocked when we heard the words "he confessed." We always silently thought, "Well, we're really screwed now." We are happy to report that these scenarios are not the end of the world. In fact they often will bolster a claim of innocence if they were done in an underhanded or illegal way.

We now know that the police and prosecutors won't hesitate to use a tainted confession when all else fails. When the state has no physical evidence, no witnesses, and not much else, watch out for the false confession. It's coming. Whenever we see confessions that are given to only one detective we're suspicious. When confessions that are not signed or do not match the case facts, look out. Whenever a confession is obtained from a juvenile outside the presence of their parents or counsel, be wary. Whenever a confession is obtained outside of the police station, like at a crime scene or back of a squad car, investigate the hell out of it.

The defense bar has caught onto this little game of false confessions. Some judges and most juries view them with suspicion. But failure to investigate the circumstances surrounding these statements is unpardonable. Without the facts there can be no resolution. Always look at these miraculous statements with a jaded eye.

Some examples from real cases that we have worked on are:

A client who was no stranger to police custody is picked up for a double homicide and is in custody for 48 hours. At no time while in custody did he speak with the detectives. In fact in, every previous incident where he was in custody, he never waived his rights. The next day while awaiting bond court he was in the courthouse lock up. His lawyer is late for court. The two sheriff's police investigators tell the bailiff to move him to a visiting room to meet with his lawyer. The bailiff moves him and the two detectives walk in. This is where the story gets murky.

One week later a police report is generated where the police allege that the client confessed to the double homicide. There is no signed statement. No witnesses other then the investigating officers and no mention of the confession at bond court that day. The client states that he never made any type of admission. Sadly a host of reviewing courts has held that this was "good enough." The client has been on Illinois death row for more than 23 years. He maintains his innocence as of this writing.

Case number two involves one that got away. Gervis Davis, a career criminal, is picked up for a double murder home invasion in Southern Illinois. At some point during his first night in custody he is taken for a ride by the local Sheriff. During the course of this ride a confession is extracted. The Sheriff's version is that Davis confessed while riding around. Davis's version was mildly different. Davis stated that while riding around in the country he was taken handcuffed from the squad car, forced to kneel on the side of the road, where the Sheriff placed his cocked and loaded .357 magnum in his ear and convinced him to confess or die right there. Davis was subsequently executed in spite of the evidence that had been brought to light in his case. Once again there was no supporting evidence to bolster the state's case.

Case number three involves Madison Hobly. Hobly was accused of setting a fire on the south side of Chicago in a multi-unit apartment building. The fire killed eight people including his wife and infant son. Hobly had no previous criminal record.

A police informant who had a long history of arsons in his background immediately identified Hobly. Hobly was taken into custody where he allegedly signed a confession. The arresting Chicago police detective stated that the written confession was destroyed after "somebody spilled coffee on it." We weren't aware that coffee has agents in it that destroy paper on contact.

During Hobly's perp walk he shouted to the camera, "I'm innocent, they are torturing me." Hobly sat on Illinois death row for 16 years before Illinois Governor George Ryan pardoned him. Hobly is the only individual that I know of who has ever been pardoned for the killing of seven people.

I could cite another fifty cases where false confessions were obtained; unfortunately there are not enough trees in the northwest to supply the paper it would require. In the alternative we would suggest that you watch out for the following danger signals when considering whether or not you may be dealing with a false confession.

- The confession does not match the known facts
- The confession was out of character for your client
- The confession was obtained outside of the custodial agencies offices

- The confession is undocumented
- The confession does not match eyewitness accounts or differs substantially
- There are allegations of physical abuse or torture
- The confession was obtained after more then three hours of questioning
- The confession was made by a juvenile
- The confession was obtained after previous attempts had failed
- The confession is denied by the client

All of these scenarios are potential goldmines of investigation. When all else fails we have seen all too often the magical confession suddenly appear. Unless the client actually tells you that the confession happened as reported or alleged, there is always room for detailed inquiry into the facts surrounding the purported confession.

## *Creatures of Habit*

Like our criminally-minded clients, the police are also comfortable with certain routines when manipulating, conjuring up or creating evidence. Like our clients they also are very much creatures of habit and custom. Our clients tend to specialize. Be it murder, burglaries or drug dealing, they tend to stick with what they know best. They are comfortable with their own particular area of expertise.

Police officers to tend to specialize and sub-specialize. Some of them are narcs for their entire career. Some work robbery, burglary or are experts at obtaining those difficult confessions or statements form non-cooperating witnesses or suspects. Over time their reputation grows. They are called in to the station to deal with witnesses that are "difficult." They have the magic touch and they produce "miraculous results."

We love the miracle workers of law enforcement, because when we run across one of these specialists we know that the game is just beginning and hopefully the meter is running. If the meter isn't running them we just have to enjoy the challenge. Where does one start when dealing with Detective Neverlost. Well, like our client, Det. Neverlost has a history and history always repeats itself.

Det. Neverlost being a creature of habit has successfully testified in many cases that are similar to your case. He has also amazingly testified in a very similar manner. Sometimes the testimony will reflect a pattern that can be considered miraculous when one is viewing several different cases. This is fertile investigative territory.

In addition, also like your client, Det. Neverlost has probably acquired a host of enemies throughout his long and distinguished career. Perhaps even amongst his brother and sister officers. Certainly amongst the criminal defense bar. Never fail to make inquiries about Det. Neverlost's miraculous powers with these folks.

There is also the area of civilian complaints and lawsuits that Det. Neverlost may have been accused of or been peripherally been involved in. Inquire with subpoenas if necessary.

### *Attacking the Formal Statement*

A videotaped statement is not the end of the world. In fact they are often the easiest to deal with. How does one go about dealing with this seemingly impossible piece of evidence? Well, we have found that one goes around to the back door and starts making inquiries about what happened prior to the goods being delivered. Therein lays the gold.

Lesson Number #1: **It** isn't what is on the tape that is necessarily critical but what happened prior to the recorder being turned on. We have personally overcome two videotaped murder confessions by attacking the credibility of how the tape was made, what was done or said to the client prior to the "taped confession" and what were the total circumstances surrounding the making of the video.

Many a shady deal has been cut with an unsophisticated defendant prior to his TV debut. A whole bunch of crazy promises are made and broken. Clients who tend to be poorly educated, mentally deficient and or trusting have made many a false statement against their best interest when making some sort of admission on video. The promise of going home as soon as you admit your involvement is commonplace. Pledges of talking to the DA and getting you probation are famous last words.

Prosecutors really dislike video. They know what goes on prior to the tape being made. They have been burned on more then one occasion when DNA tests have proven that the statement was a total fabrication. The defense bar has been insisting that videos not be used as evidence unless the entire interview and interrogation are filmed.

They are right in requesting this but for a whole host of nonsense and excuses we will never live to see the day when that happens. In the interim never give up hope because there happens to be some sort of formal written or taped statement in the case.

In the chapter on police and prosecution misconduct we delve into this area of investigation in more detail. The lesson here is that one should never overlook the abuses and fairy tales that occur in this part of the case. There is always hope.

## *Summary*

Interviews and interrogations are the bread and butter of what we do in these cases. All paths lead to this area. Be it expert witnesses, identification witnesses or occurrence witnesses, this is where the wrongful conviction investigation often fails or succeeds. Most witnesses have an agenda of some type. It seems in some cases that everybody is lying and creating. Sorting out the fact from fiction is often tedious and frustrating. In some cases it becomes downright dangerous.

Human beings are often very difficult to figure out. We have witnessed trials where multiple witnesses from both sides of the aisle have gotten on the witness stand and lied. Cops, bad guys, the lawyers, even the judge. It is mind boggling to watch. Competent detail-oriented interviews help sort out the fact from fantasy.

When the interview portion of any specific case has been weak or virtually nonexistent, the case itself tends to follow that path. We have learned one thing for certain. When the interviews and sometime interrogations are properly and professionally performed, the rest of the case tends to follow the same route.

# 7

## *Investigating & Understanding the Science Issues in Wrongful Conviction Cases*

"The thing is you don't have many suspects who are innocent of a crime. That's contradictory. If a person is innocent of crime, then he is not a suspect."

*—Edwin Meese, Attorney General*
*Of the United States, 1986*

To those of you who are reading this from behind bars for a crime that you didn't commit, you are probably numb to the nonsense that you have heard come out of prosecutors' mouths throughout your ordeal. When the Attorney General of The United States of America makes an outrageous statement such as above, the rest of us had better run for cover—because we could be next. Ed Meese is gone, and we are sad to report that his successors haven't made much of an improvement.

In this chapter we would like to assist you in exposing the mistakes and frequent abuses that law enforcement has rained down upon many a defendant's head in the name of science and justice. These abuses come in the form of what is commonly called junk science and outright perjury from medical and laboratory personnel. These abuses happen for many reasons, such as improper storage of biological-based evidence, tainted and creative testimony from prosecution experts, lost paperwork, misinterpretation of scientific data, etc. The single most overriding umbrella issue that encompasses all of this is the "Win at any cost" attitude of the law enforcement community.

The pressure starts when an individual is named as a suspect in a criminal case. The case is weak. There are no witnesses, or at the least very unreliable witnesses. There is no connection of the suspect to the crime. Much physical evidence has been collected. The CSI folks have not discovered the "magic bullet" that will connect all the dots. The police are certain they have the right guy. In all likelihood they quit thinking about alternative suspects 10 minutes after they had this suspect in custody. The blinders were put on and they stayed on. The prosecutor has held a press conference announcing, "We got the right guy." However, the "right guy" is looking more and more like the wrong guy—as there is in reality practically no evidence against him.

The defense attorney is certain they have the wrong guy. His investigator has identified an alternative suspect through a number of credible witnesses. Defense motions are being filed in batches. The media is starting to think, "Could the DA be wrong?" The DA is not happy. This is an election year. He refuses to look incompetent or, even worse yet, indecisive. He calls in the lead detective. He tells her in no uncertain terms that there had better be some great evidence getting turned up, and he wants it yesterday.

The lead detective, being no fool, realizes that her job and position are at risk. She has doubts about the case and goes to her Chief.

The Chief is a survivor of many political wars. He and the DA are old friends. The DA and the mayor are political allies. The Chief does not have to spell it out. If the DA is unhappy, the mayor becomes unhappy. If the mayor is unhappy, the chief will be retiring early. With two college kids in school he has no intention of retiring, because some mope got lucky and didn't leave his wallet at the crime scene.

The Chief thinks about this problem, and realizes that his lead detective is well educated, has worked a multitude of crimes and always preformed well. The only concern over her is that she is a civil service employee and not indebted to the mayor or DA. If the DA doesn't get re-elected she can always go back to a squad car. Nope, the Chief realizes that this matter has to be handled in a delicate and quiet matter.

The Chief's department is small. The County Sheriff's office does all of the laboratory and forensic work for the county and a host of smaller departments. The lab personnel are county employees. They have never even met the Chief. However they know the Sheriff because he signs their paychecks. He also appoints the head of the lab and determines the lab budget every year. The Sheriff and the Chief went to the police academy together, were city detectives together, and have enjoyed a friendship both personal and professional for thirty years. In fact, their wives are second cousins, not a well-known fact outside of their families.

One week later the Chief and the Sheriff are at a Republican Party fundraiser as is every politician and lawyer in town, including all the judges. This is not unusual. These functions are as normal and routine as the sun rising. The Chief after a few cocktails runs into the Sheriff, they exchange pleasantries. They inquire about one another's families, jobs, hunting season plans etc. They then do, as professionals usually do at these functions, they start talking a little shop. The Sheriff mentions that he has been following the Chief's high-profile murder investigation case closely. He congratulates the Chief on a fine job of bringing the scoundrel to justice so quickly.

The Chief thanks the Sheriff but says, "You know it's a great arrest but we're having some problems with the forensic stuff and the DA is eating my detective's ass over it." The Sheriff says, "Well you know how DA's are," and they both laugh. Nothing further is said about the matter that evening.

The next day the Sheriff has a budget meeting and the Chief of the Lab is there. After the budget meeting the Sheriff pulls the lab chief to the side and tells him that he understands that the latest and greatest murder investigation is being held back because the lab is not doing their part in bringing this scoundrel to justice. The lab chief is aware of the case and has already received dozens of phone calls from the lead detective and an assistant DA. He knows the case is weak forensically. He also knows that the Sheriff never comments on these cases. Hell, all the Sheriff cares about is getting elected, hunting and fishing and of course politicking.

However, the last time the Sheriff cared about a case was when he got embarrassed over an inmate dying under suspicious circumstances. The lab was no help at all in clearing his jail guards of any misconduct. The investigation died, but it was pretty hairy for a little while.

The lab chief suddenly lost two positions and 10 percent of his budget after that fiscal year. The Sheriff told him maybe "the state could take over all this lab nonsense, he didn't need the headache". The lab chief being no fool, and not wanting to relive that nightmare goes back to the lab and informs his staff that "if they want to be here next year, they had better get a handle on this recent high profile murder case."

A young Ph.D. lab guy who is in the meeting is really nervous. He has $90,000 in outstanding student loans; his wife is pregnant with their second child. He is low man on the totem pole and the lead detective has been abusing him on the phone. He has stuck by his moral and ethical code. He is a team player, but he isn't going to manufacture evidence.

On the other hand, the more he thinks about it the clearer it becomes. The lab chief was speaking directly to him in a round about way. He waited to get this job for two years. The economy sucks and there aren't any recruiters beating down his door. The more he thinks about it the clearer it becomes. He knows these people. They go to church together; they are honest and hard working. He is part of the law enforcement community. The lead detective hasn't asked him to do anything illegal. His boss hasn't talked to him directly. Maybe he needs to look at this blood evidence a little more closely. He doesn't get paid enough for all this grief. He isn't sleeping well.

His wife is worried about him. The pressure of this investigation is just killing him. While examining the forensic evidence for the hundredth time, he thinks that he just seen an important connection. He believes that he has just found a speck of the victim's blood on the scoundrel's NIKE tennis shoe. He calls the lead detective he tells her they have made a breakthrough. He thinks he can put the scoundrel at the crime scene. The lead detective calls the DA and she tells him that the lab has just informed her that they have hard evidence in the murder case. The DA is ecstatic. He leaks the information confidentially, to a favorite reporter. The next days headline reads, "Scoundrel's Goose is Cooked Now," in smaller letters under headline, "CSI links victim's blood to Scoundrel."

The Chief calls the Sheriff and tells him how grateful he is for the lab's great detecting work. The Sheriff replies, "No thanks necessary, they just did their job." The sheriff calls the lab chief and tells him that maybe in light of his people's recent performance the lab can get that new 220,000 dollar high fangled machine they been wanting, just like the fellas on CSI have. The lab chief calls in his young Ph.D., and congratulates him on breaking the case wide open. The Ph.D., who hasn't read the papers, is slack jawed. He knows that his testing is incomplete. Against all his ethical training he humbly accepts the lab chief's congratulations and goes back to his lab table without saying anything. He spoke to the lead detective and *told her* that the tests weren't done yet. He told her *"Don't say anything to anybody yet."* At least that is how he remembers the conversation.

The Ph.D. is sitting with a computer print out in his hands. The blood on the NIKE shoe belongs to the scoundrel, not the victim. He is sick, literally sick to his stomach. The DA, the papers, the lead detective, his boss, they all think he's a genius. He is sure of the results, hell, he has a sample of the scoundrel's blood in the refrigerator right next to his desk. He has two options; he can go tell his boss "a horrible mistake has been made." Or he can just drop one little tiny, barely visible, speck of blood on Scoundrel's NIKE. The scoundrel is black, poor and a known criminal. He has no friends. He has no future. The lead detective has told him all this. The assistant DA has confirmed it. It's not much of a choice at all. He does what he has to do.

Eight years later Scoundrel has been sitting in prison doing *hard time.* He knows somebody has lied and he is innocent. His trial attorney looked at him like he was nuts when he turned down a deal that would have got him out of jail in 12 years. The DA thought he was nuts. His Mama thought he was nuts. He is now doing life without the possibility of parole. He ain't going anywhere. Scoundrel's original defense investigator has always had a bad feeling about this case.

She was a young investigator when this case started. She had a tendency to not want to upset her clients. The client defense lawyer pulled the plug on her investigation after the DNA results came back. The judge wasn't too enthused about spending county money on a dead bang loser. The defense lawyer wasn't too excited about ticking off a judge that appointed him to a lot of cases. The client was difficult to deal with. He was mean, he was stubborn, and he wouldn't listen to reason. The client's own family didn't even like him. The lab wouldn't make this stuff up. They were scientists, not cops.

She had seen a lot in the last eight years. The Ph.D. guy from the lab was now a star. When things got tough he got to testifying. When he testified the state always won. He was known as the "miracle worker." Other jurisdictions sought him out to "assist" in their own tough cases. His reputation was booming, he was *"The man."* She figured he was slick. She thought, "The man my ass, more like the whore." She liked the old client a hell of a lot more then she liked the scientist. In fact she always had a feeling about this client. She always thought that she wouldn't be a whole lot nicer then he was, if she'd been locked up for a murder she didn't do. The more she thought about it the madder she got. In fact, she was starting to think, that maybe the client was telling the truth. The only problem was how in the world she could prove it.

## DNA

DNA (also known as deoxyribonucleic acid) is the genetic material present in the nucleus of cells in all living organisms. DNA has been called the "blueprint of life," since it contains all of the information required to make an organism grow and develop. The majority of the DNA is identical from one human to another, but there are locations in the DNA that have been found to differ from one individual to another with the exception of identical twins.

These are the regions of DNA that are analyzed and used to compare the DNA obtained from an unknown evidence sample to the DNA of a known individual in identification testing.

Because each individual inherited half of his or her DNA from each parent, DNA testing can be used to determine if individuals are genetically related to each other. DNA is found in all cells with a nucleus and is in the same throughout the body, so virtually every fluid or tissue from a human contains some DNA and can be analyzed by DNA identification testing. DNA also is stable and does not change over time, so samples collected years ago may be compared to samples collected recently.

There are three types of DNA. Listed below are the types and their uses:

### Restriction Fragment Length Polymorphism Testing

RFLP testing is the most widely used method. RFLP testing generally requires that a sample contain DNA that is not degraded (broken into smaller fragments) from 100,000 or more cells (e.g., a dime sized or larger saturated blood stain). Smaller samples are not suitable for RFLP testing but are used in PCR testing.

## Polymerase Chain Reaction Testing—Nuclear DNA

PCR testing of nuclear DNA as it is commonly used in forensic testing laboratories may be done on a wide variety of samples that are quite small, containing 50 to 100 cells or more (e.g., visible dot of blood, a single hair root.) PCR is the test method of choice for samples that contain DNA that is degraded (e.g., pathology specimens, samples that have been improperly stored or are aged).

## Polymerase Chain Reaction Testing—Mitochondrial DNA

DNA contained in the mitochondrial (an organelle involved in producing energy) of cells can be isolated and the sequence of the DNA bases can be determined. Mitochondrial DNA testing is generally performed on samples that is unsuitable for RFLP or PCR testing of nuclear DNA, such as dried bones or teeth, hair shafts, or any other samples that contain very little or highly degraded DNA.

## Historical Information

All this DNA stuff is up until recently one of those areas that only a few select people understood. It took a while for all of us to understand DNA's impact on the criminal justice system. We now know that DNA has been the single biggest reason that many of the wrongfully convicted have regained their freedom. It has been a magnificent tool for the fight against injustice. However it is not the only avenue open to the wrongfully convicted and their quest for freedom.

In 1986, in its first known use of DNA testing to solve a criminal identification, Colin Pitchfork's DNA was matched by multilocus RFLP testing to the DNA from semen from two rape/homicides in Naborrough, England. Before Pitchfork was identified, a 17-year-old mentally challenged mental hospital kitchen porter, who had confessed to one of the murders, was released after 3½ months in custody when the DNA results showed the same person raped both girls eliminated the kitchen porter as the source of the semen. Although homicide detectives originally thought the DNA evidence contradicting the confession was "bloody outrageous," the kitchen porter was released based on the same work of the same people who had put him in custody.

For at least seventeen years we have had the miracle of DNA to assist in the fight against wrongful convictions. As chronicled by Attorneys Barry Scheck & Peter Neufeld in their book *Actual Innocence*, DNA has been the savoir of well over

100 men who had been wrongfully convicted. Scheck & Neufeld are the undisputed masters of DNA and their book is the finest that I have seen on this subject. With regards to Junk Science/Sloppy Science, they make the following recommendations:

The underlying scientific basis for many forensic tests must be objectively reevaluated under the standards enunciated in recent Supreme Court decisions designed to keep junk science out of court.

Microscopic hair-comparison evidence should be abandoned. Instead **mitochonical** DNA testing of hairs should be conducted in any hair evaluation involving a matter of importance

Like medical labs, all the disciplines in crime labs should be subjected to regulatory oversight and should meet standards of professional organizations. States should create agencies modeled after New York's Forensic Science review Commission—an independent panel composed of scientists, prosecutors, defense counsel, crime lab directors, police and judges-that have real authority to provide effective regulation of laboratories.

All crime laboratories must be accredited. This is not a panacea but a good first step. Accreditation should improve rigorous quality control and quality assurance review, periodic inspections, and spot-checking of technicians data.

Laboratories must submit to a rigorous proficiency testing program, including blind testing, in which samples would be sent in and analyzed as though they were part of an ordinary case. Labs should be rated on their ability to come up with valid results.

In court scientists should provide, as matter of course information about "controls" and whether they failed; and what the error rate is for procedure.

Defense lawyers should have all material scientific evidence independently scrutinized, if not retested, by a competent expert. Public defenders and court appointed lawyers must have funds to retain qualified independent experts.

Every public defender's office should have at least one lawyer who acts as a full time forensic science specialist helping other lawyers on their cases

## Investigation

Scheck & Neufeld's recommendations cut right to the heart of the matter of junk science. Based on these recommendations we would recommend that either through Freedom of Information Requests or Subpoenas that the above information and policies from each individual lab that you have contact with be verified and investigated fully. It does not matter when the tests were conducted. It could have been last month or ten years ago. Your job is to find out what was the condition in which the lab was being operated at the time of your relevant test(s).

An outfit called the International Standards Organization does the most reliable and strictest certification that a lab can undergo. This group inspects all labs that are not forensic-related. It is a strict and detailed audit. If a lab is ISO certified, then they are in compliance with accepted scientific standards. We would suggest you contact ISO and get a copy of their protocol.

The American Society of Crime Laboratory Directors inspects forensic labs. This all sounds very official when flowing forth from a lab director's mouth on the witness stand but try and obtain a copy of their inspection/certification report and it's unavailable. The inspections are conducted in a two-part phase.

An individual who comes out and insures that the lab has the appropriate documents in place does the initial inspection. Then another inspector comes out and makes sure the documents are all there. If they are the lab is certified. In short this is a fairly worthless process, which means nothing.

When investigating the lab we would recommend that the following documents either be subpoenaed or a freedom of information request be filed seeking their production:

- Any and all outside inspections or audits done on your lab during the period in question.
- All internal audits and inspections conducted internally.
- A list of all personnel who assisted in or conducted tests in your case.
- Copies of CVs or résumé of above personal.
- A copy of the lab protocol with regards to whatever tests were being conducted.

- (If you do not already have this) A copy of the technicians or scientist's raw notes.

- Any and all memos issued to law enforcement on the handling, packaging and shipping of evidence to the lab.

- Any and all disciplinary actions or files on (the employees who did the testing/comparing in your case.

- Conduct full Internet, nexus, Lexus search on lab and personnel.

- Conduct complete background investigations on all involved lab personnel.

## Fred Zain

Fred Zain is the poster child of law enforcement in wrongful conviction cases. If not for the diligent and, in retrospect, brilliant work done by a public defender named George Castelle, Zain would still be sitting on witness stands across the southeast and falsely testifying in criminal cases. It was Castelle's work in one such murder case that exposed Zain. We won't rehash the entire matter here, but instead will reprint excerpts from another excellent book titled *Wrongly Convicted: Perspectives of Failed Justice.*

With regards to Fred Zain's role in wrongful conviction cases, The West Virginia Supreme Court of Appeals summarized what it described as Zain's "long history of falsifying evidence" in criminal prosecutions:

The acts of misconduct on the part of Zain included 1) overstating the strength of the results; 2) overstating the frequency of genetic matches on individual pieces of evidence; 3) misreporting of genetic matches on multiple pieces of evidence; 4) reporting that multiple items had been tested when only a single item had been tested; 5) reporting inconclusive results as conclusive; 6) repeatedly altering laboratory results; 7) grouping results to create the erroneous impression that genetic markers had been obtained from all samples tested; 8) failing to report conflicting results; 9) failing to conduct or to report conducting additional testing to resolve conflicting results; 10) implying a match with a suspect when testing supported only a match with the victim; 11) reporting scientifically impossible or improbable results.

In a 1993 deposition that Attorney Castelle conducted on West Virginia State Trooper Investigators Sabrina Gayle Midkiff and former State trooper Lynn Inman (Moreland) the following exchanges took place:

Q. *(George Castelle)* How many did you see that were clear cut where (Fred Zain) appeared to be making up results that didn't exist?

A. I couldn't give you a number. It's a large number though.

Q. I won't put words in your mouth, but to give us a better understanding, by large, would that be 10 or 20 or 100 or 1000?

A. Probably, considering over the period of time, it may be close to 100. It became routine, and it got to the point where I didn't pay any attention.

Both Trooper Midkiff and Trooper Inman testified in the 1993 investigation that they reported the fraud to Zain's state police supervisors and showed them examples of the fraud, yet the supervisors continued to praise Zain and recommend him for promotions. Trooper Inman stated:

> A: Our complaint was that [Zain] was calling things that weren't there. Then I really felt it was kind of up to the supervisors to take a look at that.
> Q: Did you discuss it with the supervisors?
> A: Yes sir, we did...
> Q: And what did they do?
> I don't know. Nothing was changed.

A review of Zain's personnel file during the period of time in question confirms Troopers Midkiff and Inman's disappointment in Zain's supervisors. His evaluations during and after the time the complaints read as follows: "Sergeant Zain will go beyond what is normally required to assist field investigators and to keep the backlog down to a minimum in this section. Sergeant Zain is continually attempting to improve advanced Serology techniques in this section." (West Virginia State Police personnel file of state trooper Fred S. Zain, semi-annual evaluation report, 1 January-30 June 1985), "Continues to demonstrate a high level of job interest. Level of productivity is excellent in the Serology Section." (Semi-annual evaluation report, 1 January-30 June 1986) "An efficient run section, Sgt. Zain continues to demonstrate a high level of job interest in the field of serology. He goes the extra step when trying to assist the investigator and prosecutor." (Semi-annual evaluation report, 1 July-31 December 1987; "Recommend for promotion" (semi-annual evaluation report, 1 January-30 June 1988).

The Zain nightmare was responsible for human misery that is truly immeasurable. In addition to Zain's activities his supervisors were aware of the misconduct, perjury and illegal activities. Not only did they not discipline or refer him for criminal charges, they continued to protect and promote him. Sadly Zain is not even the worse of the known offenders of this type of activity. However, once again space prohibits us from chronicling more misconduct.

Checking back in with our defense investigator, she has been looking at all the possibilities of how to go about saving Scoundrel. She has attempted to speak with the Chef who is now retired and living out of state. When she finally does contact him, he says he doesn't remember any details. "I know Scoundrel did it, so I never give it any thought." The Sheriff is now a judge. He doesn't recall the case either and tells her, "I never had anything to do with the lab, "they were a pain in my backside."

The lead detective is now chief. She and the DA got married and are the power couple in town. She tells the defense investigator, that Scoundrel was "guilty as hell." She refuses to comment further, pending litigation and all that.

The young Ph.D. lab guy is now a renowned scientist. He, like Fred Zain, was a hero to everyone in law enforcement. The entire defense bar smells a rat, but is paralyzed to do anything…They've tried and gotten nowhere. Our defense investigator starts at the beginning. She has nowhere else to turn. She goes to the courthouse in an adjoining county and finds the Ph.D. expert's fairly common last name listed as a defendant in a paternity suit. She isn't sure it's him; she orders a bunch of files out of storage. She treks back repeatedly over the next few months, files lost, misplaced, clerks to busy. She is tired of it all, but yet she still has a feeling.

After 3 months and more than one hundred hours of work, she comes across the file. It is empty except for a complaint that was filed pro se. She thinks it's against the Ph.D., but there isn't enough information to be sure, the document is a copy and a bad one at that. She seriously thinks she should move on, another dead end. She decides to give it a shot. She eventually locates the complainant who is in rehab and homeless. Another six months go by. She realizes what a long shot she's dealing with. The Ph.D. is long married, a pillar of the community, stable family. Not a hint of scandal. Blah, blah, blah, she is really getting sick of all this free no-paying work.

She enters the rehab clinic finds the complainant from the file. She has AIDS. Has been homeless, continues to stumble through life. She is distrustful of the defense investigator. She initially refuses to talk to her; she is hostile, uncooperative, and not interested in giving history lessons. The defense investigator spends several hours with her, tells her some of her "man problems". The AIDS/rehab patient warms up. She tells her she wasn't always in such bad shape. She brags about being very attractive at one point in her life. She tells her that the Ph.D. is definitely the same guy that is in the paternity suit. She tells her she filed the suit, but lost interest. She let it die and gave up the kid to a relative.

Tells her a remarkable yet extremely detailed story about an affair she had with the Ph.D. She tells the investigator that he is a liar, a dishonest person. The investigator says, "Did he lie about fathering your baby" The woman tells her no, he lied about some dude named Scoundrel; put him in jail for life. The woman says that the Ph.D. and she had an affair and his nerves were shot at the time, from work pressure. He told her all about Scoundrel. The woman has a remarkable memory for details. She agrees to give an affidavit.

Six months later Scoundrel walks out of jail into his family's arms. No one believed him for over eight years. He sat and he rotted in jail and no one listened. Not the courts, not his lawyers certainly not the system. The system fell apart. He was saved by one stubborn and determined defense investigator. It was her actions that did it. In reality after the adverse affidavit came to life so did the defense bar, the media, the courts? A concerted effort by all, a superhuman effort. But the linchpin of the whole case was the investigator's stubborn streak and instincts. Let that sink in when you've seemingly run out of options.

### Summary & Conclusion

The outlook for you overcoming lab misconduct, mismanagement, and just plain old sloppy unprofessional work is frankly bleak. The state has been able to convince most judges and the respective legislatures that inquiries into a specific laboratory's inner workings are unnecessary. Judges have repeatedly stated that it is "irrelevant." The Illinois Supreme Court enacted a rule in 2001 that helps you get to the heart of the issue, but only with regard to DNA testing.

We will repeat what the rule reads below, however the defense bar would certainly like to see this rule be applied more liberally across the board. In any event it makes for an excellent guide when seeking production of relevant documents and information.

Reprinted form Illinois supreme Court Rules, adapted March 1, 2001

Rule 417. DNA Evidence

a.  Statement of Purpose. This rule is promulgated to produce uniformly sufficient information to allow a proper, well informed and determination of the admissibility of DNA evidence and to insure that such evidence is presented completely and intelligibly. The rule is designed to provide a minimum standard for compliance concerning DNA evidence, and is not intended to limit the production and discovery of material information.

b.  Obligation to Produce. In all felony prosecutions, post-trial and post-conviction proceedings, the proponent of the DNA evidence whether prosecution or defense, shall provide or otherwise make available to the adverse party all relevant materials including, but not limited to the following:

   (i) Copies of the case file including all reports, memorandums, notes, phone logs, contamination reports, and data relating to the testing in the case.

   (ii) Copies of any autoradiographs, humigraphics, DQ Alpha Polymarker strips, PCR gel photographs, and electropherogams, tabular data, electronic files and other data needed for full evaluation of DNA profiles produced and an opportunity to examine the originals, if requested.

   (iii) Copies of any records reflecting compliance with quality control guidelines or standards employed during the testing process utilized in this case.

   (iv) Copies of DNA laboratory procedure manuals, DNA testing protocols, DNA quality assurance guidelines or standards, and DNA validation studies.

   (v) Proficiency testing results, proof of continuing professional education, current curriculum vitae and job description for examiners, or analysts and technicians, involved in the testing and analysis of DNA evidence in the case.

(vi) Reports explaining any discrepancies in the testing, observed defects or laboratory errors in the particular case, as well as the reasons for those and the effects thereof.

(vii) Copies of all chain of custody documents for each item of evidence subjected to DNA testing.

(viii) A statement by the testing laboratory setting forth the method used to calculate the statistical probabilities in the case.

(ix) Copies of the allele frequencies or database for each locus examined.

(x) A list of all commercial or in house software programs used in the DNA testing including the name of the software program, manufacturer and version used in the case.

(xi) Copies of all DNA laboratory audits relating to the laboratory performing the particular tests.

The above looks like it was written by some yellow dog Democrat.

The question is why aren't we entitled to this in every lab function that is performed? Well it may be a Supreme Court Rule in Illinois, but we just spent two years fighting the state to get just a little of this info in an ongoing wrongful conviction case. The circuit court refused to enforce part or all of it. We had to seek relief from the Supreme Court before we finally got some of it. The point being is that it is never easy. If you get any of the above, you will be lucky.

We could never give adequate coverage to all of the misconduct that occurs in the police laboratories in this country. We are just now starting to scratch the surface. We could have provided you with nightmare stories concerning GSR tests (gunshot residue test), fingerprinting, voice analysis, drug testing etc. Hopefully you got the point. Simply stated, always verify, never trust. The outrageous misconduct that often occurs is often not so much outrageous, as it is below the surface. It is subtle, quiet and unknown to most. Now you know. Your job is to never ignore the possibility of it happening to your client.

# 8

# *Laboratory Abuse, Misconduct &*
# *Fraud*

*"The first and wisest of them all professed,*
*To know this only, that he nothing knew.".*

—Socrates
*Paradise Regained*
*IV, 1. 293*

This chapter is an afterthought. I had originally thought that the DNA chapter would cover this entire subject. It didn't and thus I was forced to do this one. When I was preparing the outline of this book, I did not give this subject much thought in spite of the fact that I have been following the trail of criminal misconduct by laboratory analysts and so called scientist for years.

I first became aware of this issue when a public defender in West Virginia (George Castelle) took apart the lab in Richmond and specifically a man named Fred Zain. Mr. Castelle's efforts really shined the light on this nonsense and he was one of the first to really expose the lab abuse that routinely occurs.

Consequently, a true scientist and former FBI agent by the name of Fred Whitehurst single handedly wrecked the FBI lab in Washington D.C. and caused those folks years of grief for their arrogance and apathy towards justice. Dr. Whitehurst has since quit the FBI, successfully sued them, and has a whole new career exposing lab fraud throughout the United States.

Since then I have come across a number of people who are heroes by virtue of their work in exposing misconduct and fraud by the government's sacred cow which is commonly referred to as Forensic Science.

Television has created a significant problem for us in that they have glorified the police lab with the never ending fairy tale of CSI. Scientists are portrayed as the all knowing, all seeing brilliant, but quirky, know it alls, who solve a crime in 45 minutes or less. Their toys (lab equipment) are beyond reproach. They are honorable and they never lie. Excuse me while I vomit.

Crime labs, fingerprint experts, arson investigators, firearm ID experts and the like are the bane of the criminal defense bar's existence. They have very little creditability, and hardly any scientific qualifications. The problem with bad science or what we refer to as "junk science" has reached catastrophic and biblical disaster proportions. There is good and bad news for those of us trolling in the trenches.

The good news is, is that we in the defense community have or at least should have discovered a whole new area of fertile investigation which can be quite complicated and time consuming. The bad news is that we have just increased our work load by 1000 percent.

The courts have traditionally shown blind confidence in anyone who comes into the courthouse proclaiming to be any expert in any discipline. Throw some sort of law enforcement or academic credential in the mix and we have people proclaiming to be experts in *Elbow Prints.* Yes, ladies and gentleman we have elbow experts amongst us and you didn't even know it.

In addition, the courts have routinely bought into this nonsense and regrettably to a large extent we have gone along with the program. Our clients have gone off to the gallows and we were left wondering what happened in there?

What happened was we got caught with our pants around our ankles. Like the courts we (the criminal defense bar) have been woefully unprepared, lazy, or just incompetent in exposing these fairy tales. Due, to budget restraints, poor planning or just general laziness, we have been getting our collective asses kicked by the government when Mr. Wizard hits the witness stand.

Like the 7$^{th}$ grade biology class who oohs and aahs when the science teacher drops an egg into a beer bottle without breaking the egg, we have been hoodwinked into sitting and watching the quote forensic expert explain, "elbow prints, bite marks, lip prints," and other fairy tales. We sit their and the jury who is generally far more gullible then us, flushes our client right down the toilet. We then walk out of the court and stumble around and bitch about the unfairness of it.

Frankly this chapter should be a book. This material is lengthy and complicated. So, I will do what all good authors do. I will steal the great work of others and print it here. Clearly, most folks ignore the foot notes and will give me credit for others hard work. However, against all self interest, I am begging you to read and note the footnotes because that is the material you should be digesting.

I am merely trying to get your attention and lead you to the significant stuff that has been written about this subject. If you are still with me, you can skip the rest of this chapter and go right to the resource page of this chapter. If not, hang in there for a few more pages and then copy the resource page and call up those folks and bug them.

### *Forensic Science a.k.a. Forensic Nonsense*

If you are like me, you have generally bought into the infallibility of science. Add the word *forensic* to science and you have a pretty snappy description that has fooled some pretty smart people in our business. I have always been a proponent of investigating any and all experts. I have written, published and given dozens of speeches on the subject. And, I have been doing it for a very long time.

However, where I and many of my brethren have fallen short is in investigating the science and not paying close enough attention to what these so called, self proclaimed experts were saying. Big mistake and I pray no one is sitting in the shitter because I did not *fully investigate* what these experts were actually claiming to be fact.

In the DNA chapter, we talked about problems with DNA analysis and a specific case. We make some recommendations and site some specific actions. However, DNA is just a very small but famous part of this equation.

Forensic Science has laid claim to the following area of expertise:

- Fingerprints
- Tool marks
- Ballistics

- Blood Spatter
- Serology
- Identification
- Fibers
- Arson & Explosives
- Toxicology

The above disciplines are accepted as fairly routine and unquestioned. Once again a big mistake, but listed below are some of the *new* areas that the local forensic genius is taking claim to:

- *Lip Prints*
- *Elbow Prints*
- *Footprint Analysis*
- *Bite Marks*
- *Voice Prints*

We can accuse the state of much, but not being creative in new theories of science is not one of them. Whenever we plug one hole in the dam three others appear. In this case, the *"Forensic Scientists"* keep coming up with new and creative ways to hammer someone when there is no other substantial evidence. This phenomenon is called, "winning at any cost."

The first thing that you must know in order to combat this nonsense is the difference between a scientist and a technician. We have allowed the government to blur the two and promote them as the same animal. They both may be dog's but the similarities end there.

A real scientist will possess a legitimate Ph.D. A lab technician or forensic examiners will often only posses nothing more then a bachelor's degree or even an associate's decree. Tool mark, firearm, fingerprint, handwriting, etc., experts will often start working as police officer, transfer to the lab, move up thru the ranks and become a scientist thru Immaculate Conception. It's amazing but their qualifications are often boiled down to, *"I have been a fingerprint examiner for twenty two years"*.

That's it. Think about that for a second. Some state anointed expert gets up on a witness stand and simply states that he has been reading, comparing analyzing fingerprints for a period of time and the whole room accepts his qualifications as something that has been sent down from the mountain top.

### *The Crime Lab*

Now that I have gotten your attention about the self anointed experts that launch your clients into the penitentiary, let's examine where they actually work. This bastion of science is often referred to as, *Forensic Science Laboratories.* That is a pretty damn impressive name, but it is often anything but that.

In the United States there are 285 crime labs that are actually accredited. Accreditation is only gotten thru the American Society of Crime Laboratory Directors. Out of the 500 or so crime labs out there a little more then half are actually accredited by their own people. What's up with the other half? I would venture to guess that if they can't get their own people to accredit them, they are in serious trouble.

Throughout this book, I have steered away from giving attorneys any legal advice. This is a practical guide on how to attack the case and investigation, not a legal treatise. However, I can't help myself, so here is as close as I will get to giving advice to my brethren in the bar;

*Do not under any circumstances stipulate to scientific state generated evidence and the results of same.*

Having been burned more times then I can recount here, I am begging you if you're reading this, don't stipulate. The state (all of them) have proven time and time again that they cannot be trusted to not mishandle, misdiagnose, or flat out lie about evidence.

For example, in the most comprehensive article that I have seen written on this subject former FBI Agent Fred Whitehurst recommends that you seek the following in your initial discovery request from the state.

- Evidence collection forms or logs (description of evidence, packaging, identification of specimens, identification of individuals collecting samples, sample collection procedures).
- Chain of Custody records. (field-to-lab transfers and all transfers of evidence and associated analytical samples within the laboratory).

- Laboratory receiving records. (records documenting the date, time, and condition of the evidence in question; laboratory assigned identifiers; storage location).

- Laboratory procedures for sub sampling (collection of analytical aliquots) and contamination control.

- Copies of technical procedures in effect at the time the subject testing was performed (often termed Standard Operating Procedures, or SOP's) for each procedure used during screening and confirmation, including; sample analysis, data reporting, and instrument operation.

- Copies of two bracketing controlled substance proficiency results for each analysis of subject specimens, including; raw data and reported results, target values and acceptance ranges, performance scores, and all related correspondence.

- Copies of traceability documentation for standards and reference materials used during analysis, including unique identifications, origins, dates of preparation and use, composition and concentration of prepared materials, certifications or traceability records from suppliers, assigned shelf lives and storage conditions.

- Sample preparation records, including dated and conditions of preparation, responsible analyst, procedural reference, purity, concentration and origins of solvents, reagents, and control material prepared and used, samples processed concurrently, extract volume.

- Copies of bench notes, log books, and any other records pertaining to case samples or instruments; records documenting observations, notations, or measurements regarding case testing.

- Instrument run log with identification of all standards, reference materials, sample blanks, rinses, and controls analyzed during the day/shift with subject samples (as appropriate: run sequence, origins, time of analysis and aborted run sequences).

- Record of instrument operating conditions and criteria for variables, including as appropriate: gas chromatograph column, instrument file identification, tuning criteria, instrument performance check (e.g. ion abundance criteria), initial calibration, continuing calibration checks, calibration verification.

- Record of instrument maintenance status and activities for instruments used in subject testing, documenting routine and as needed maintenance activities in the weeks surrounding subject testing.

- Raw data for the complete sequence (opening and closing quality control included) that includes the subject samples. For GC-MS analysis, this would include: areas and retention times, injection volumes, dilution factors, chromatograms and mass spectra. As prepared and as determined values for all quality control samples.

- A description of the library used for spectral matches for the purpose of qualitative identification of controlled substances, including sources and number of reference spectra.

- Copy of records documenting computation of illicit drug laboratory's theoretical production yield, including the basis for the computation, and the algorithm used, as appropriate.

- Procedure(s) for operation and calibration checks of analytical balances used to weigh controlled substances.

- Results of calibration checks and documentation of mass traceability for gravimetric determinations.

- Results of contamination control surveys for trace levels analyses relevant to test methods at the time of analysis, including sampling design and analytical procedures.

- Records and results of internal reviews of subject data. (these are generally peer review reports)

- Method validation records documenting the laboratory's performance characteristics for qualitative identification and quantitative determinations of the controlled substance, to include data documenting specificity, accuracy, precision, linearity, and method detection limits.

- Copy of the laboratory's Quality manual in effect at the time the subject samples were tested as well as the laboratory's most recent Quality Manual (however named; the document that describes the laboratory's quality objects and policies).

- Copy of the laboratory's ASCLD-LAB application for accreditation; and most recent Annual Accreditation Review Report, as appropriate.

- Statement of qualifications of each analyst and/or technician responsible for processing case samples to include all names, locations and jurisdiction of cases in which these personnel testified concerning the same substance in the present case.

- Copy of the laboratory's ASCLD-LAB on site inspection report, as appropriate, as well as any reports of on site inspections by any other testing laboratory audit organization.

- Copy of internal audit reports generated during the period subject samples were tested.

- List of all capitol instrumentation in the laboratory at the time subject testing was performed, including manufacturer, model number, and major accessories.

- Production throughput data for the drug testing section: numbers of tests performed per month or per year, and the number of Full Time Equivalent personnel in the drug testing section of the laboratory.

Whitehurst also explains in his article as to why and how these materials are critical. This is litigation at its most complicated. Do yourself a favor and find someone who can actually understand all of these materials. This should not be left up to anyone on the team who struggles with science.

This area of investigation is perhaps the most overlooked and consequently our collective Achilles heel when investigating the wrongful conviction. The material is difficult, the language unfamiliar, the process puzzling to the layman. Like all other complicated areas that we must learn when defending clients, this specific issue is something that we just have to master.

This is all just part of solving the puzzle. Very often we will be doing an initial exam of a specific case and we will be looking at perhaps two witnesses who claim that the defendant told them "I did the murder." The defendant is of course denying ever making any statement of the kind. Fair enough. We see that every day.

We then start to look at the fingerprint evidence. Bad. Really bad. His prints are all over the crime scene and he denies ever being within twenty miles of it. Fifteen years ago we would have packed it in after reviewing that evidence, or at least the transcript from the trial and the testimony of the state or FBI expert. We would have told the defendant, sorry, we can't help you, generally believing that the government would not have dared lie about something so easily verified.

Well, we have come a long way since then. In 1997 the New York State Police fabricated testimony with regard to fingerprints in more than forty cases. This is just one example of forensic fraud. At the time of this writing, we suspect that there is a whole host of fraudulent activity not yet discovered

The forensic science community has seemingly been hoodwinking us for years. Just as there are many honest and ethical police officers out there, we have hundreds of ethical and eminently qualified scientists and lab personnel. There is my disclaimer. Now that I have said it, let me state unequivocally that when a lab expert of any kind gets on a witness stand in this country and lies, manipulates tweaks or creates evidence in any manner, they need to go to jail. I'm living to see that moment. I haven't heard of it happening yet, but I'm waiting.

Here is the main issue in a nut shell. The forensic science community is in turmoil and getting in deeper every day. They haven't really established a structural agency that is properly funded or regulated. Combine that with a death penalty system that is very much out of control and we have the perfect recipe for disaster. It's been happening; it is happening now and will continue to happen for years to come. All we can do as criminal defense practitioners is to continue to question and investigate the process closely.

I have borrowed heavily from the two experts in this area Fred Whitehurst and Craig Cooley. Both of them are fairly interesting people to say the least. Both started their careers as investigators. Both are now licensed attorneys. Whitehurst is in private practice in North Carolina, and Cooley is with the Federal Defenders Habeas Unit in Las Vegas. Cooley and Whitehurst decided to become attorneys because they were fed up with how attorneys were just basically ignoring the forensic evidence. Both of them are brilliant in this area and they enjoy the entire defense community's collective endorsement.

If you find yourself in a case where scientific evidence/testimony is an issue, get in touch with either one of these experts. They may save your clients life and they most certainly are comfortable, knowledgeable and expert with science and forensic issues.

# 9

## *Police & Prosecutorial Misconduct as a Defense Investigation Strategy*

*"In government offices which are sensitive to the vehemence and passion of mass sentiment public men have no tenure. They are in effect perpetual office seekers, always on trial for their political lives, always required to court their restless constituents."*

—*Walter Lippmann, Essays in the public philosophy [1935]*

As a private investigator that specializes in criminal defense and catastrophic personal injury cases, I had thought that after 21 years in this business, I thought I would see a decline in police and prosecution misconduct. Misconduct is defined as *to manage badly or dishonestly.* What it should be called is misdeed, which is defined as *a wrong or wicked act.* We are saddened to report that police and prosecutorial misconduct is alive and well in America, and it is indeed wicked.

This chapter is designed to wake up those among us who believe that prosecutorial and police misconduct is rare or isolated incidents with regards to the prosecution of the innocent.

Clearly, the vast majority of criminal cases that are brought to trial are worthy. But, just as clearly, there are a substantial number of cases (especially murder, sexual assault, and child abuse) that are brought to trial with little or no evidence. Many of these prosecutions are political in nature. States or district attorneys, who are getting ready to run for re-election or seek the next higher office in the political totem pole, love what we call in Chicago a *"Heater case."* Heater cases always involve high drama, and lots of press. Unfortunately "heater cases" bring out the worst in the police and local prosecutors office.

These are the cases where a rush to judgment is made. These are the cases where if obvious mistakes were made by the police, the police refuse to re-examine or take a second look. These are the cases where political careers are made and lost. These are the cases where book and movie contracts rights are won, where television careers are launched. These are the cases where a defendant's civil rights are the last thing considered. In short, these are the cases that the criminal defense team will spend years undoing the damage that has occurred.

Having been involved in more than thirty wrongful conviction cases there is not one instance that police or prosecutorial misconduct did not play a major part. Defendants were beaten and tortured into confessing to a crime that they didn't commit. Witnesses were threatened and harassed into making a false identification, or giving perjured testimony from the witness stand.

Physical evidence disappeared or was lied about from the witness stand; the deplorable use of jailhouse snitches bolstered a weak case; the hit parade goes on and on.

Yet, try to remember the last time a prosecutor or police office was punished for participating, creating or being a part of a government sanctioned conspiracy to convict an individual.

The vast majority of police officers, prosecutors and other government agents are honest, hardworking, dedicated and committed to playing by the rules. They will play by the rules whether they agree with the rules or not. They will do it because if they don't they have just become what they are arresting or prosecuting—a criminal.

Having said that, we find ourselves increasingly faced with a case involving misconduct on the part of the police, the prosecutor, or both. It is no longer an isolated incident that only happens in large urban areas. It happens everywhere, regardless of population, geography or size of one's office. The reasons that it continues to grow are not surprising.

We have been electing demagogues who make "The Crime Problem" their number one priority. The stepping stone to higher office is that you must be tough on crime. Consequently, we have more laws on the books then any country in the world. We have seen the federal criminal code rewritten so that sentencing could be fairer. Nothing could be further from the truth. In fact a number of Federal Judges have revolted in protest.

More than one hundred people have been released from the death rows throughout the United States. However, this only happened after battles that raged for years throughout the court system were fought. They were not released because a police officer, detective or prosecutor decided, "that they had the wrong guy," they were not released because a lone individual came forward with newly discovered evidence.

In the overwhelming majority they were released due to a well orchestrated team of professionals usually working pro bono, and usually in concert with a major news organization(s) blasting the state nightly on the evening news, or writing a string of stinging and condemning articles about the case in chief.

In short, the courts responded to the public embarrassment of having locked up the wrong person and finally (usually after many years), reluctantly released the individual with normally no apology or compensation. (See the system does work!)

This chapter is directed at the number one cause of these wrongful convictions: *police and prosecutorial misconduct.* Most wrongful convictions have two other root causes, ineffective assistance of counsel and no or ineffective investigation.

**Number two, police officers, laboratory's technicians, district attorneys, state or government experts committing perjury or manipulating evidence and or witnesses to obtain the desired result, a conviction.**

Volumes have been written about the first problem, which is ineffective representation. Suffice to say that if counsel weren't ineffective, the misconduct would have likely been discovered at trial. However due to inexperience, lack of funds and a hundred other reasons, that are all too common it is not discovered. But, just as often the misconduct is so well concealed that counsel is unaware of the problem.

If you have been sailing off of the waters of southern Antarctica for the last 70 or 80 years, perhaps you have not heard of some of the issues that have plagued

American law enforcement and its related entities. The following historical perspective should help bring you up to speed.

Because Chicago is the center of the universe and the Granddaddy of modern corruption and misconduct, we'll start there.

In author Gus Russo's book called *The Outfit,* Russo details the history of organized crime and the corruption and buying of Mayors, Governors, Judges, Alderman, State's Attorney's, and of course the police.

Russo details the buying and selling of virtually every government official/ employee from 1850 through today. In 1850, when Chicago had more than 80,000 citizens, there were only *nine* "city watch marshals" and no police department. Bookmakers, thieves, and pimps started fixing and engineering elections as early as 1879 when Mayor Carter Harrison "sold" the bookmaking concession to an Irish gangster named Mike McDonald. Ironically, the Chicago Police Department's highest award for valor is called "The Carter Harrison Award." Somebody had a sense of humor.

In 1900, when Chicago achieved a population of 2.1 million people, the police department numbered 1,100. A 1927 study counted 1,313 gangs, which had more than 25,000 active members. Comparatively speaking the gang problem today is a shadow of its former self.

From early in its history until the late 1980s, Chicago's criminal element virtually ran the political and judicial system in Cook County. They slated and elected judges. They rigged political races wherever their interest lay. They were widely believed to be responsible for the election of President John F. Kennedy. They were able to accomplish this through their stranglehold on virtually every labor union in the country.

In Cook County, which is the nation's largest county court system, more than 80 policemen, judges, lawyers, and court personnel were indicted and with the exception of a very few all were convicted and for the most part sent to prison.

In James Touhy and Rob Warden's 1989 book *Greylord, Justice Chicago Style,* Warden and Touhy chronicle the long term selling and buying of Justice in Chicago. The justice department's investigation named Operation Greylord, which was the largest and most comprehensive corruption investigation of all time.

In May of 2002, Chicago Police Department Retired Chief of Detectives and highly decorated Police Captain William Hanhardt received a fifteen year federal prison sentence for organizing, running and participating in a jewel theft ring. Some of his co-defendants and partners were mafia hit men. And if you think that Chief Hanhardt was only trying to supplement his meager $80,000-a-year retirement, (he keeps the pension), think again.

Chief Hanhardt was on the mob payroll long before he retired. FBI agents testifying at sentencing indicated that the chief, kept his mob buddies apprised of any federal or city investigation into their activities throughout his long career.

Affidavits submitted in Federal court quote Ken Eto, former mob gambling boss, former victim of three gunshots to the head by off-duty Cook County Sheriff's policemen. (Their part-time occupation was paid hit men for the Outfit.) Eto survived due to faulty ammunition. The Sheriff Deputy's did not survive. For bungling the assassination the two Sheriff Deputies became "trunk music." Mob slang for, being found shot and dead at the O'Hare International Airport parking garage.

That is the second most famous thing for which O'Hare is known. The first is that it's the world's busiest airport. Eto is a current guest of federal government, (witness protection program). Eto stated that he personally paid Hanhardt money to ensure favorable treatment of Eto's gambling operations.

Speaking of O'Hare airport, it is named after Navy Lt. Butch O'Hare who won the Congressional Medal of Honor in WWII. Butch attended the Naval Academy at Annapolis and was a true war hero and all around great guy. However, his Father Edward "Artful Eddie" O'Hare was a business partner and confidant of Al Capone's in a number of dog racing tracks.

O'Hare senior became an invaluable government informant. O'Hare was the person who informed the judge in Capone's income tax trial that all of jurors in the Capone's tax evasion case had been bribed. The judge then brought in a jury pool from out of town that in short did what the entire Chicago Police Department could not or would not do, and that is convict Capone and send him to prison.

For O'Hare's cooperation with the government he was shot and murdered while driving his car. The murder was thought to be a "gift" for Capone upon his release from prison.

So even though Lt O'Hare's act of heroism was described by President Roosevelt as "one of the most, if not the most daring single action in the history of aviation," corruption has managed to tarnish the O'Hare name.

Getting back to Chief Hanhardt, Robert G. Siegel, a one time associate of Hanhardt, was quoted as telling agents in 1967 that Hanhardt was receiving "$1,200 a month and a new car every two years".

U.S. Attorney Scott Lassar stated, *"Hanhardt's organization surpasses in duration and sophistication just about any other jewelry theft ring we've seen in federal law enforcement, said Mr. Lassar. "The defendants would determine the most opportune time to steal jewelry from places such as cars and hotel rooms by surveiling traveling salesman and by keeping detailed records analyzing their routines, all with the purpose of providing income to themselves from the stolen property."*

The total take of the theft ring was estimated to be $4.8 million dollars. At sentencing Hanhardt was unapologetic.

Then we have high ranking member of the Conservative Vice Lords street gang, Edward Lee "Pacman" Jackson. Jackson received a 115-year sentence for ripping off drug dealers for cash and drugs, intimidating witnesses and conspired with crooked Chicago police officers all while (surprise, surprise) working as a Chicago Police officer himself. Jackson, who was a social sort of fellow, and a strong believer in sharing the wealth, was sentenced along with six other Chicago Police officers, known as the Austin Seven in October of 2001.

It may have started in Chicago, but New York is second to nobody. In the late 1800s we have New York City Police Department Chief Inspector Alexander "Clubber" Williams. (Wonder how he got the nickname, Clubber?) Old Clubber was brought up on charges no fewer then 358 times but was never dismissed or even apparently disciplined, and who was so magnificently talented at corruption that by the time of retirement he had accumulated a yacht, a house in Connecticut, and savings of $300,000.

Onto the sunshine state we have the elite Delta squad out of Manatee County in Florida. These law enforcement professionals, four of them to date, have plead guilty to a variety of federal charges, which resulted in more than 100 criminal charges being dropped against 67 separate defendants.

They robbed drug dealers, they beat them, and then they bragged about it. Some of the crimes they committed were: bogus search warrants, placing crack cocaine on witnesses to ensure cooperation, seizing cars and property without evidence of wrongdoing, and stealing cash.

Deputy U.S. Attorney Jeffrey Del Fuoco stated that the officers "way of doing things seemed fairly entrenched." Del Fuoco also stated that he expected further charges. It's unclear, he said how far up the chain of command the improprieties go.

Then there is Hartford Connecticut Patrol Officer Julio Comacho. Comacho admitted in court that "he handcuffed a woman, drove her in his cruiser to a construction site and raped her over the trunk of his patrol car." Comacho is also the prime suspect in Rosa Delgado's murder. Seems that Delgado was Camacho's former girlfriend. She was murdered and beheaded. The couple's four-year-old daughter is still missing. Want to guess who the prime suspect is?

In 1999, the FBI was openly investigating the Hartford officer's connection to at least three murders, including the Delgado case.

Speaking of the FBI, Former Director Louis Freeh, stated in a speech in 1998 *"No law enforcement agency, and certainly not the FBI is immune from the scourge of corruption. We have arrested FBI Special Agents, and obtained convictions, on a variety of charges."*

Director Freeh went on to say that, *"in recent years the FBI has arrested police officers for corruption in every region of the nation, in large medium-sized and small cities, towns and villages; from the inner city precincts to rural sheriff's departments."*

If you believe that the FBI is generally free and clear of any misconduct, other then to what they openly admit, let's consider a little scandal that was brought to Congress' attention by Special Agent Fred Whitehurst. SA/Dr. Whitehurst,

Whitehusrt has a Ph.D. from Duke University and was the FBI's biggest headache since Bobby Kennedy tried to figure out how to get rid of J. Edgar Hoover.

Whitehurst had the unmitigated gall to internally complain about the FBI's crime lab irregularities. When Whitehurst complained through the chain of command and his superiors, they first attempted to have him declared mentally unfit. When that failed they fired him and slandered him. Unfortunately for the FBI, Whitehurst was unimpressed with their efforts. His congressional testimony rocked the criminal justice system.

Eventually the FBI let Whitehurst retire and, oh yeah, they wrote him a check for over one million dollars for his trouble. All Whitehurst ever wanted was scientific honesty from the lab personnel and their supervisors. What he got for his trouble was his own private hell of terror provided by the world's most respected law enforcement organization.

In Los Angeles, the city of angels' police department recently suffered through perhaps their worst case of corruption to date. Considering their history, that in itself is quite a statement. LAPD's Rampart Division was accused of having a network of conspiracy that planted evidence, lied repeatedly at thousands of trials, committed murder, and basically ignored every law that was on the books. This scandal resulted in over three thousands cases being overturned.

In May of 2002 the Hong Kong police chief was arrested along with a senior police inspector, and a detective station sergeant for accepting free prostitution services for tipping off nightclubs about impending police raids.

In 1998, the FBI arrested three Detroit police officers for conspiring to commit a robbery of approximately $1 million.

In Starr County, Texas, the sheriff, a justice of the peace, and five county jailers were charged with bribery and conspiracy to commit bribery. In the same year nine current or former West New York, New Jersey police officers were charged with racketeering involving protection of prostitution and illegal gambling.

If the reader believes these to be isolated incidents, sorry, they are not. Sadly the Chicago Police Department and just about every major police department in the United States have suffered through scandal after scandal after scandal. Contract killings for organized crime, drug dealing, organized burglary and jewel theft rings, the planting of evidence on police shooting victims, the crime wave by those who swear to protect and serve is continuous and never-ending.

All of the aforementioned documented incidents are outrageous. The law enforcement community would have one believe that they are isolated incidents. But, as criminal defense professionals know, as do the authorities, criminals get caught after having usually committed dozens if not hundreds of criminal acts. We will never know the true depth of the problem.

However what the criminal defense bar is slowly but surely understanding is that police corruption and prosecution misconduct start at the bottom. That is to say that long before a scandal erupts detailing drug dealing, murders, bad police shootings, claims of torture etc., other bad acts start creeping in.

What are these bad acts? Well, for starters the mentality that has been around since the beginning of time that allows police and prosecutors to put on evidence that they know is false or misleading but impossible to prove. This is done in every courthouse in every jurisdiction in the world. The mind set seems to be that, "Hey we're just removing another criminal from society." What's the problem? You have to bend the rules to get the desired result, right?

Judges know it, juries know it, and the defendants know it. Yet we are seemingly powerless to stop it. So after you have waded through the last ten pages or so, you are now fooled into believing that the author is finally getting to the point of this chapter. Well maybe.

After having been involved in literally thousands of criminal investigations, we have found the silver bullet or magic formula that will help you to become a more complete investigator or litigator is quite simple.

Investigate your opponents. Really, it is that simple. If you are involved with litigation on a criminal defense level you have a professional and moral obligation to investigate the people that you are up against. To not do it is unpardonable.

Where does one start? Well one starts where he is sitting, at the courthouse. Many years ago much to the dismay of anyone who has ever been involved in any litigation, somebody decided to make available to the public: court records. What a novel idea. One can actually go to The Clerk of The Circuit Court, provide the clerk with a name, and viola, a record of some sort shows up. Contained in that file are all types of interesting information.

Now, public officials, police officers, lawyers of all types, and any other self-anointed VIPs really dislike this nonsense usually called the open records act.

They really dislike it because in the unlikely event, that they have ever been in trouble or come to the attention of some government agency in some location in the world, their name and dirty laundry is right there in black and white, along with all the sordid details chronicling their bad behavior. Well as professionals we know that sometimes these reports are like the funnies in the Sunday paper. Very entertaining but not a lot of substance.

In the event that a record does exist, you are only as good as the information that can be independently verified through interviews, other documents, and different sources of information.

So what kind of records should one seek when they are looking for this sort of information? Well, the first rule should be; never overlook criminal record checks because the person you are investigating is law enforcement affiliated. The tendency is to not check because you think that law enforcement personnel or those in sensitive positions have already been screened.

As with all things in life, there are many variables. For example in Chicago, NBC television reporter Dave Savini recently checked every police, fireman & paramedic's criminal history. What he found was that more than 100 hundred police officers had arrest and convictions for battery, driving under the influence, assault or domestic violence. All of the police officers were on active duty and working. Why weren't they discovered prior to the NBC piece?

The answer is, of course, nobody checked. The firemen and paramedics fared even worse. Now, being of a more liberal bend, I would say live and let live. However, we are dealing with people who have the potential to make statements from the witness stand that will often launch your client into the bowels of the nearest penitentiary. If these statements are questionable or outright fabrications, you may have wished that you had checked their background prior to trial.

Where else do we want to find information? Well as a general rule, the civil section of the clerks' office at the court house is an excellent choice. The civil division will have all kinds of interesting data. Domestic Relations also known as divorce court will maintain a record of every divorce ever gotten in the county in question. Who will know more about a former spouse's dirty laundry then an ex-spouse?

Allegations of child abuse, non-support, orders of protection, accusations of drug and alcohol abuse. This is a depository of allegations that will make The National Enquirer blush. As with every other bit of information you collect this should always be verified. Remember you are almost always dealing with mere allegations. You gain nothing by acting irresponsibly.

Also listed in the civil division are lawsuits filed by and against your target. Never overlook this most important aspect of intelligence gathering. Has the subject been experiencing severe financial difficulties recently? Has he or she been living outside of their means? Are they involved in some kind of insurance scam involving stolen property or vehicular accidents? Are the subjects "moonlighting" in a business with a conflict or potential conflict of interest? Are close family members or associates involved in any questionable or unethical schemes or illegal activities?

The possibilities are only limited by your ability to conduct thorough complete searches. This is not a simple matter of one sending down the client's wife or significant other to conduct the research. This is a complicated business involving a host of endless jurisdictional possibilities: federal, state, county, city and township. Every state is different and the nuances are sometimes so subtle an amateur will miss them.

You may be saying to yourself that this is all fine with police personnel, but what about investigating opposing counsel? My God, we're gentleman (or ladies as the case may be) lawyers don't investigate lawyers. Shame on you. Those unwritten rules died with Clarence Darrow. Prosecutors have and continue to investigate defense counsel routinely. Just because you are unaware of it doesn't mean that it does not occur.

As with police and prosecutors, defense attorneys have been known on occasion to break the law or act inappropriately. Because one is in possession of a law degree, does not mean that one will always be on their best behavior.

Assuming that lawyers are a little more self-disciplined and they manage to stay out of the courthouse as a client, there are many other avenues of inquiry. The local Attorney Registration and Disciplinary Commission has a file room full of material that has a wealth of fascinating reading. This is of course where attorneys get complaints filed against them by clients, former clients, really ticked off judges, other attorneys they have wronged, widows, orphans, and ex-wives, or anyone else they have managed to make angry, sleep with, steal from, and or act in an unprofessional manner.

In addition to the state or local bar association, one should never overlook opposing counsel's involvement in other litigation. As with lazy police officers that rewrite the same complaint for search warrants over and over again, lawyers are creatures of habit as well. Pleadings, depositions, trial transcripts, will almost always at the very least indicate and predict how opposing counsel may act under any given situation. It becomes very obvious early on in your research when you see a pattern of abuse or inappropriate conduct.

Along with this mountain of paper that you are searching there is always the thing that works when all else fails. Gossip. Yes, gossip is the start of all good rumors.

And, nobody loves great gossip better then cops, lawyers, inmates and court personnel. If these people weren't interested in everybody's business they would be working at a real job where they could make a real contribution to society.

So when all else fails ask someone about somebody. If you ask enough people you will hear something bad. If you hear something good (or in our case something malicious or mean spirited) then you may be onto something. All great cases start with rumor, innuendo and bullshit.

Finally, for those of you who are still kicking and screaming about having to use the Internet or anything computer related, let us make one final plea at convincing you that this is a valuable skill for one to possess. If you enjoy making money, you'd better start liking it. The Internet is a place where any moron with a second grade education can write anything they want about anybody.

Often it is garbage in and garbage out, but just as often it is a gold mine of information. It is a good place to start your investigation about your target. As with all other sources of information, it always needs to be verified independently.

Police and prosecutorial misconduct are not always obviously present. Often they are not obvious at all, in fact usually it is subtle and well hidden. The process of unearthing it is always tedious and slow. More often than not, it does not lead you into the next super scandal. But, you would be remiss in your duties if you didn't consider the possibility that it is occurring in your case.

Now that we have regaled you with specific instances of misconduct and criminal acts we would suggest that when you suspect that misconduct has become an issue in your case, the authorities will likely call it incompetence, rather than criminal misconduct. Be that as it may, if you committed acts of misconduct on this scale there would be little doubt that your name would appear on some judge's docket as a defendant.

With that in mind, we would be remiss if we did not caution you against utilizing this tactic unless you are absolutely certain that you can prove misconduct or gross negligence on the part of the authorities. Once you start down this particular slippery slope, there is no climbing back.

As we have already addressed informal sources of information, we would like to examine how you would attempt to gather records through a more formal means. At some point in any wrongful conviction case, you will hopefully obtain subpoena power. With this very powerful tool at your disposal we would recommend that if police misconduct has become an issue you start utilizing them.

One of the first subpoenas issued will be to the subject(s) own department. The language in this subpoena should read something like this:

*Any and all personnel, training, disciplinary records on Detective John Neverlost to include; Civilian complaint forms, Police & Fire Board hearings or complaints, Internal Affairs Investigation Reports, memos, photographs or any other materials which reflect any allegations of misconduct or formal inter-departmental disciplinary hear-*

ings to include suspensions, termination proceedings, or letters of misconduct or memorandums detailing any allegations or formal proceedings. Also requested are all
training, police academy records, and any other documents which reflect human
resource files to include job evaluations or any other documentation kept in the normal course of business.
*This is not a request for personal information such as; date of births, home addresses or
social security numbers. Please delete all references to the above.*

When this subpoena is served it will receive a lot of attention. The state will be
filing motions to quash. The judge will want to know why this information
should be turned over to a defendant, etc. It has been our experience that most of
the time the judge will allow some of the materials to be turned over. Often they
will want to do an in camera review to see if any of the subpoenaed information is
relevant to your case.

These subpoenas succeed far more often then they fail. You will never know
when an officer or detective has fallen out of favor with his or her own department. If we have learned one lesson it is that when an officer is very active he or
she makes enemies in and outside of their departments. We have also received
calls form other police officers that have heard from one source or another about
a subpoena of this nature being issued. They have provided other avenues of
investigation due to their dislike of the officer in question.

## Snitches & informants

We could have written an entire book on this section alone, and indeed dozens of
articles have been written on the subject, so we will keep our comments brief with
regards to this particular class of animal. Actually animal is probably too kind a
term as this species is all too often beyond description.

When discussing snitches and informants we are referring to the ones that for
whatever reason agrees to cooperate with a prosecutor or law enforcement agency
against an innocent criminal defendant. We are not talking about the usual
snitch that is running down to the courthouse to cut a deal against a co-defen-
dant. The years have taught us that 99 percent of the population will rat, snitch
or cooperate to save themselves. If you do this long enough, you will eventually
represent a person who is "cutting a deal." Honor among thieves has been a thing
of the past for many years now. It is virtually nonexistent.

We are directing our comments against the individual who volunteers or becomes a jail house snitch in a case that he or she has had no involvement in until they either volunteered or were recruited by a member of the prosecution to "help them out".

Fortunately for your client this is the easiest it's ever going to get for him or her. It won't be easy, because the government will go to extreme measures to protect this snitch that is until they no longer require their services. They will then toss them like used Kleenex.

In the interim, there are just oodles of fertile detecting tools available to you. Listed below for your convenience is a list of areas to look into.

- Police Informant files (subpoena required)
- Police payment records
- Prosecution Deal memos
- Jail visiting records
- Prison/jail intelligence files
- Prison/jail disciplinary records and hearings
- All prior arrest reports from every agency you can locate
- Always get copies of old mug shots
- Any psychiatric or psychological test results from schools and correctional institutions
- Any medical records from any institution
- Transcripts from old trials, hearings and depositions
- Military records
- Job & personnel records

You will also want to do the general background investigation that you would conduct on any prosecution witness. Statement should be obtained from the following sources:

- Any past victims of criminal acts committed by snitch
- Any former law enforcement personnel who arrested snitch previously

- Ex-wives and girlfriends
- Past attorneys who represented snitch in other matters
- Family members (They often dislike the snitch more then your client)
- Past cellmates
- Correctional personnel from other institutions that snitch has been housed in
- Old Employers and supervisors
- Other victims of similar behavior

All of the above is a starting point. You are only limited by your imagination. The thing with informants and snitches is that they usually have been doing it for a long time. Their enemy's list is usually long and very bitter. In addition they will almost always brag about how much *they hate snitches and informants.* When you start taking statements from and subpoenaing old victims and fans to the courthouse, the snitch's usefulness as an informant or reliable witness is greatly diminished.

In almost every occasion that we have revealed police or prosecutorial misconduct the use of a snitch or planted informant has come up. The two seem to go hand in hand. The relationship between law enforcement personnel and informants is almost always inappropriate.

The longer the relationship, the more chance for the snitch or informant to get his law enforcement handlers in trouble. We have seen law enforcement allow snitches to deal drugs, commit murders and lie under every conceivable circumstance. This relationship almost always has baggage.

## Summary

The professional courtesies extended to law enforcement personnel by the defense team ceases to exist when gross misconduct or illegal activities are discovered. The turning of one's head and ignoring or not commenting on official's misconduct stops when your innocent client has been or shortly will be railroaded into the penitentiary.

Because one wears a badge or is appointed or elected to prosecute criminals, one does not get a pass on being a criminal or conducting themselves outside the boundaries of the law. We realize that law enforcement has a mostly thankless job.

We know that many of them are honest, hardworking and diligent in the performance of their official duties. We also know that in the vast majority of wrongful conviction cases that we have been involved in, law enforcement has acted irresponsibly and with reckless disregard for our client's rights. When that occurs the sun must be shined upon those activities. If they have acted within the parameters of their office, police and prosecutorial misconduct will not be the issue.

# 10

## *Dealing with Satan*
## *Or*
## *How To Mange a Media War In The Wrongful Conviction Case*

*"We will not be driven by fear into an age of unreason if we...remember that we are not descended from fearful men, not from men who feared to write, to speak, to associate and to defend causes which were, for the most part unpopular."*

*—Edward R. Murrow*
*See It Now (broadcast). Report on Senator Joseph R. McCarthy [March 7, 1954]*

Why has the United States with these gigantic twin chips on its shoulder named morality and fairness and a claim to moral leadership of the world gone entirely in the opposite direction? Why does well over half of the American public support the death penalty? Did we learn nothing from history? From slavery? From lynching? Indian massacres? It wouldn't appear so. In keeping company with the excellent examples of fairness and democracy in places like North Korea, Iran, Yemen and other forward like thinking countries we continue to murder our citizens in spite of overwhelming evidence that we have; A) Killed innocent men; B) Proven unequivocally that the death penalty is racist and arbitrary.

Why has this phenomenon persisted in spite of the best efforts of generations of Americans who has fought the death penalty? Mostly it has continued because the media in general has stood by and reported, but has taken an overwhelmingly neutral stance of not complaining about it. The lesson here folks, is that the media could make it go away. They could rail against and bring unbearable pressure on the politicians who support it. But they won't because death sells, and the more violent and dramatic the death, the bigger the story.

For the most part in this text we have nagged you about paying attention to individuals who receive a sentence other then the death penalty, but the fact is, the Chicago Tribune will not put something on the front page that is not death penalty related. We are immune to long sentences. The general public will not pay attention to it for more then five minutes. The newsroom editors and television reporters know it and we know it.

As a result, when the media does get interested, look out. If your client is guilty, the trial is usually over with by the third or fourth bad TV or newspaper story. Put a fork in him or her, they are done. The smaller the town, the more significant the media influence. Conversely when the media gets interested in a wrongful conviction story and reports on it favorably, you have won half the battle. The trick is of course is to get them interested, keep them interested and most importantly get them to think like you.

This is a lot easier said then done. Our colleagues in the police and prosecutors office are absolute masters of self promotion.

While we were busy filing motions in the courthouse for a bond, they were on the front steps of the courthouse firing the first salvo of artillery fire straight into the bowels of your case. They were lined up, dressed well, standing in front a set of flags gently blowing in the breeze.

Who cares what the hell they were telling the media, damn it they looked great! While every reporter in town (both print & television) was out there drooling over every spoken word, silly you was actually working diligently.

Shame on you. You have just dug your client such a deep hole; he or she may never dig themselves out. If you don't listen to anything else that we have told you in this text, now is the time to wake up and get with the program. Because, when you find yourself trying to undo fifteen years of damage that your client has received, you had better be ready to make some new friends.

Your new friends are going to be what was once commonly known as the 4th estate. I've forgotten what the first three are, I think government and industry are in there, but their first three estates are not going to help you influence the public and the courts. These 4<sup>th</sup> estate folks are what is now known as "the media." The media can break your back or walk your client into your waiting little sound bite embrace. The later is preferred over the first option.

In the type of case that we find ourselves normally entrenched with, we usually have a number of components that the media salivates over. We have blood, lots of tears, and usually a whole load of drama. "If it bleeds it leads." "If it weeps, we leap." The media is starved for excitement. You can only do so many consumer rip off stories. They love sex and murder more then they love a fat expense account and a number two pencil. For a while they will love your client if he or she is interesting. For a while they will love you if you help them. At some point they will turn on you like a rabid possum.

The hard lessons in life that we learn, always come back to haunt us if we fail to learn from our mistakes. We guess that is why they call them "hard lessons." Working successfully with the media is one of those hard lessons. Most of you will run away from media contact as quickly as you can. You've been betrayed by a reporter and burned badly. You want nothing to do with them. We understand. However if you are operating under a deadline and we would consider the situation of an innocent client in jail a huge deadline, we would respectfully suggest that you learn how to live with and work with the media.

The author has been blessed in his association with amazingly talented and driven media people throughout the years. We have had front row seats to their influence and power. Quite often they have been the impetus behind any given wrongful conviction case. Their stories have without question been the motivating factor behind the success of a number of the wrongfully convicted reversals. Their talent and heart have often made the difference.

When Illinois Governor George Ryan issued a blanket moratorium to Illinois death row inmates he specifically cited the media and their work as one of his main reasons for doing so. We always suspected that the judges and politicians were very much aware and influenced by the media's "take" on any given case but, for the first time we actually had a powerful politician admit to it in a very public way.

We have heard judges state from the bench on any number of occasions, "*I could care less what was on TV last night or what was in the morning paper.*" We've heard that frequently and in many different jurisdictions form many different judges. The truth though, is quite different. They do indeed watch it. They read it and most importantly, they play to it. Judges can make all the statements they want about their carefree attitude about media reports. They infrequently issue gag orders prohibiting media contact. But, at the end of the day judges are just like any other politician, except they wear a robe to work everyday.

We have had the pleasure of meeting and getting to know a number of judges over the years, and to a person they have indicated to us that they are hugely influenced by the media. Not one of them has ever stated that they have ruled one way or the other because of the media slant, but to a person they recognized and paid close attention to what was being written and reported. More importantly, their bosses, be it the Chief judge or County Board President, were always following the media closely and warning them about political or professional consequences should they do something that would cause them or their bosses any embarrassment. We have been also told by judges that members of their family almost always pay close attention to what is happening with the media coverage and aren't afraid to comment about it often and quite vocally. If you were under the impression that judges don't pay attention to intense media coverage, you may want to reconsider your position.

## Racial Considerations & Other Scary Thoughts

When playing with fire, it is wise to consider one very important factor. Is your client truly innocent? If he or she has baggage, e.g. a long and tarnished criminal history, was involved in the crime in some other matter other then the one for which he got himself locked up, or is generally a very difficult person to get along with, keep him away from the media.

Here is another consideration, and we will take a lot of heat for this one: If the client is anything other then a Caucasian, he may not be a good media story. That is unless he went to an Ivy League school, was a professional athlete, is a millionaire or a public figure. Being white will also cut him a lot of slack if he has a criminal background or is just your run-of-the-mill disagreeable asshole. Yes, race is a huge consideration from the media perspective. If you believe that statement to be false; you have probably never dealt with a TV producer, unless he or she was from BET (Black Entertainment Network) where race is an issue as well.

The above rule is void if the victim in your case was white. Then we have a racial component. For media purposes that's a good thing. Simply put, black on black, Hispanic on Hispanic, Native American on Native American and so forth does not generally receive the attention it should receive. That is the nature of this particular beast and it is not likely to change in the foreseeable future.

For those of you still doubting this theory, an example is as follows. A five-year-old white, blue-eyed, blond little girl is found beaten to death in her home. The alcoholic father quickly confesses to the crime. Now, the media will have that story lead not one night, but probably the rest of the week. There will be specials about alcoholism in the suburbs. The father will be viewed as a victim of his many life pressures who "snapped." There will be special bank accounts set up for scholarship funds. There will be crisis intervention workers at her school counseling kids for as long as necessary. We guarantee you that this story will be on for as long as the media can flash the victim's picture and get all teary eyed and weepy.

Now, scenario number two. A five-year-old black girl who lives in a housing project in the inner city is raped and beaten to death by her crack addicted mother's boyfriend. There will be outraged stories that night on the news about the crack epidemic in the ghetto. There will be a very different tone expressed towards the mother. She will be treated as a defendant, although she wasn't even present. There will be no fundraisers. There will be no follow-up stories. The prosecutor will definitely seek the death penalty against the boyfriend. To be sure the full weight of the law will descend upon the victims' house and neighborhood. The story will be dead by the second day.

Is the media racist and insensitive? Probably not. It is largely a matter of ratings and demographics? You better believe it is. It's not fair, but it is simply the way it is. If you are white you will probably strongly disagree with these examples. Before you do, ask the opinion of one of your colleagues who is not Caucasian. We guarantee you that they will know exactly what we are trying to convey to you.

We mention all of this as to not to aggravate you, but to try and educate you on the realities of this whole issue of media. Not all cases will get the attention they deserve. If you have been in this business for more then a week, you already know this. We are trying to teach you the many lessons that we have learned the "hard way". If you are still struggling with this theory, all you have to do is look at the statistics for who gets the death penalty.

A study done by Law Professor David Baldus from the University of Iowa examined 2,484 murders in Georgia in the 1970s. The study breaks down by race and who got the death penalty and who didn't.

Black defendant and white victim: 22%
White defendant and white victim:  8%
Black defendant and black victim:  1%
White defendant and black victim:  3%

Although there has been no formal studies done on the volume of media attention any particular crime gets, and any racially biased component we would be willing to bet the ranch that if there were, the statistics would play out pretty much the way they did above, if we were comparing the media's coverage. When you are considering involving the media in a case you have to consider the racial component, it is always present.

## Picking Your Media Person

There are many considerations when you are on your vision quest to find a media person who is going to help your case. They are not in the phone book or on the Internet. They are generally not parked down at the courthouse hanging out, waiting for you to call. No, this is not going to be as easy as it sounds. But, before you find this genius that is going to help save your client's life, you have to have a plan.

First and foremost do you have a good story here? Is your client interesting? Who is going to be the media contact person? Do you need the media to get your client out of prison? Can it be done without the media's attention? Is it too late to turn the media around in your case? Are they already too entrenched in the prosecutor's office? The considerations are numerous. It's an important decision. The team has thought it through and they all agree, "We need the media."

The first issue that we will always consider is, what is the writer or reporter's track record in these cases? We always want to know what kind of person is going to do this story justice. How do we go about finding this person? There are a number of referral sources to help you when making your decision. We would suggest you start here:

- Use someone you are familiar with.
- Call your colleagues, ask who they would use.
- Check old stories that are similar to yours (find an individual, who writes or reports fairly).
- Ask a friendly, uninvolved judge who they would call.

You have now identified a target and you have set up a meeting with a writer, TV reporter or producer. This meeting should be held somewhere besides their office. You will want to have prepared for this meeting like you would for an important interview. Basically you are selling something here, and you may only have one chance to sell it. You are attempting to sell this media person on the fact that your client is innocent and that you need their help in proving their innocence.

An ethical and honest reporter is not going to jump for joy at this opportunity. They are going to be very leery of your motives. They will be extremely skeptical. That's a good thing. They need to see for themselves that your client is innocent. They are not just going to take your word for it. Before they will help your client they have to believe in him or her.

This is a very delicate process. Sometimes when the evidence against your client is virtually nonexistent, it becomes an easy sell. When there is seemingly a lot of evidence, even if most of it is of the fairy tale type, it's a tougher sale.

Here is what we look for when we're picking our media contact(s)

- Are they bright?
- Do they catch on quickly?
- Are they motivated by the story?
- Are they advocates for real justice?
- Can they make things happen in their own organization? (Can they get the story printed or on the air)
- Will they be easy to work with?

- Will they understand that you have to abide by certain rules, laws, and court orders?
- Are they talented enough to do the story justice?

These are the issues that you have to think about. Giving the story to just any writer or producer will not do. They can quickly do more harm then good. This first step is the most critical step in the process. Choose wisely.

This brings us to the very delicate matter of whether or not to let the client and the media meet and get together. To gain the media full cooperation this is going to have to happen. Now clients being clients, this is always a potential nightmare for a hundred different reasons. Look at it like this; you would not let a client testify without a lot of preparation. The same holds true with the media. Rule number one. They never meet alone. You or somebody that you designate is always present when a meeting takes place. Rule number two. The client must not get into the habit of calling the reporter collect and having "off-the-record" conversations. As we have been reminded on more then one occasion by reporters, "you are always on the record."

## Type of Media

Newspaper reporters are the most likely people you will be dealing with. They usually have both the time and the space to devote to your story. Newspapers are a lot like baseball leagues. At the bottom you have single A ball. Small markets young and newer players. Not much attendance (circulation). AA ball a little bigger, the players (reporters) little more sophisticated and savvy. AAA ball, just below major league level.

The papers or TV market usually covers a wide area. Reporters are usually very good. Finally the major leagues. Big markets like Chicago, Boston, Miami, New York, etc. Reporters are the best and brightest in industry, well paid and very competitive.

They have the ability to make or break a case quickly.

Always be on the look out for an exceptionally bright reporter that may be buried in some unlikely place. Due to a host of possible reasons this reporter for whatever reason is tolling away at some small market media outlet. Or perhaps you find a really bright young reporter who is ambitious and just looking for the right story. Whatever the reason this individual could wind up being a great find. Don't discount somebody because they are in the minor leagues.

The same rules apply to the television people. The higher up the food chain, the more exposure and clout. The stakes are also higher as the higher you get the more competition for the story. If you intentionally freeze a reporter out of the story, they may very well take an adverse position against your client. This is real tight rope you are walking, so precede with caution.

Relationships with the media seldom turn into warm fuzzy little ta ta's where the two of you start attending each other's weddings. Sometimes but not often. For the most part the relationship remains at arms length. That's ok. It has to remain professional, but on the other level it has to be established and a level of trust should exist between you and the media contact. With that in mind try and remember these ground rules:

- Never lie, always be forthright
- Establish ground rules early, i.e., what documents if any you can give to the media source, what's off-the-record and what is a must have for them
- Never accept money from the media
- Never make a deal you can't produce. Don't make empty promises.
- Never do anything that you aren't willing to testify to in front of a grand jury. You have no privilege in these dealings nor does your client.

We all have felt the heat of a pissed off DA for doing our job. It is not a pleasant place to be. The media can help protect you from this.

As the DA will never or almost never attack a reporter, they will also leave you be, if they know the media is firmly in your corner. They will also not send some really ticked off cops out to have that all too familiar chat with a witness who has just flipped, if the media is involved with that witness. The last thing the DA wants to read is how his goons terrorized a witness who was just trying to be truthful.

For example I was involved in a very high profile eighteen year old wrongful conviction case where CBS network news was doing a lengthy detailed story on it. Every time we found a new witness who was critical we would do the following:

First, we would get a detailed written or videotaped statement outside the presence of the media. We would then put the witness and the correspondent together for an on camera interview. This one two punch was devastating to the state.

Not only were we able to properly document what the witness had to say, but also the story unfolded as fast as the investigation did. The witnesses were left largely unmolested by the state. The judge hearing the case realized that this case was suddenly a very high profile case and as a result we were able to move the case along at warp speed.

The defendant was released from death row in record time. CBS news had a great story, and we were largely left unmolested, not totally but enough so that we could get it done.

### Shock & Awe

In addition to lobbing guided missiles into old Saddam's latest hang out every minute for a week there are other ways to get one's target audience's attention. The shock and awe that one wishes to accomplish with a well orchestrated media blitz will include both the print and TV mediums. This is never easy as you are now dealing with a host of personalities and egomaniacs. Everyone wants the exclusive, but when the story starts getting big, that isn't going to happen.

Hitting the other side with devastating daily newspaper accounts and nightly television "investigative" pieces is devastating. This is to be employed in a manner that cumulates with an important event like a hearing or beginning of new trial. If your timing is off, it is all wasted. It is only effective when it brings heat down on the authorities. They are experts at weathering storms, so the timing of the shock & awe campaign has to be near perfect.

This is why when you are assisting the media with leads or information; you never give them everything in your arsenal at once. You must feed it to them piecemeal so that it is a continuing running drama that holds everyone's attention. This is a continuing story that has to be paced and kept interesting. It must build to a big ending. If the story becomes boring or routine you will lose any momentum that you have gained.

This is when reporters start wandering outside of your camp to find the other story. The other story is never a good thing for you. The other story will always conflict or damage your story. To avoid a rash of wandering you always have to pay attention to what is going on.

This is not a time for you to be worrying about your golf or tennis game. Paying attention means that you are doing the little things. Lots of phone calls, meetings whatever it takes you keep your media people interested in your version. The shock and awe aspect only helps your client when all of the media is attacking the state's case. Dissention is bad. Try to keep everyone happy.

## Small Town Media

Most of the reporters who cover the crime issues in sparsely populated areas are on good to great terms with local law enforcement and the prosecutor's office. They have to be because the majority of their information (stories) is given to them directly by these people. In fact if these people get mad at them, they can and will put them out of business. They simply do it by not talking to them any further. The Sheriff or Prosecutor is their main source and they will not attack or embarrass them for any reason.

This can hurt your ability to gather any positive media coverage, no matter how wronged your client is. The only way to combat this problem is to bring in outside media. Outside media can be a national news network or a nearby large city newspaper or magazine writer. Once they start writing stories that embarrass or bring into question their fairness, they may come around, but in all probability you will only neutralize the negative coverage you were receiving. Always be ultra cautious when dealing with the small town media. Their general attitude is, I have to live here with these people and you are only here for one story. They will and do leek information to the other side.

## Summary & Conclusion

Very often the success that your client will enjoy or not, will directly correlate to your ability to get the job done with the media. It's not fair, but neither is life in general. Your ability to establish rapport with reporters and get a story told that is consistent with the defense theme is critical. In fact more often then not, it won't get done without the media taking a high level of interest in the story. It's not fair or right. It is simply how it is.

There is an unofficial rule in the media. If you get built up, you get to get burned down in magnificent and creative ways. Our friends in the media love conflict. Good vs. Evil. Nice vs. Mean. Dumb vs. Brilliant. Right vs. Wrong. In Chicago for example, if the Chicago Tribune writes something nice about you, look out. The Chicago Sun-Times (the Trib's main competition) will write something equally horrible about you next week. TV shows on different channels do the same.

No matter what the level of competition in any given environment, you will get whipped up on occasionally. I would love to give you some great advice on how to avoid this. I could, but it would be a lie. This rule is as firm as the sun rising in the east tomorrow. Not if, but when.

We jokingly refer to the media as "Satan" in the title of this chapter. That is really an insult to the devil, so we should explain. If you mismanage this portion of a wrongful conviction case, you will have been happy to have Satan involved. Bad reporters can do just as much harm to your case as bad cops or evil prosecutors. Involving the media wrongful conviction case is a lot like opening Pandora's Box. You never know what's inside.

# 11

## *Summary & Conclusions*

*"Out of the Mud comes the Lotus Blossom"*

—*From Old Buddhist writings*

Old Buddha had some great sayings and we would be wise to remember a few of them. The above quote says volumes about wrongful conviction cases. Whenever you are handed or agree to become involved in a wrongful conviction case, you are as they say down at the joint, "really steppin' off into it." The highs in these cases are astronomically high. The lows will have you in psychotherapy for years to come.

The key in any wrongful conviction case, as in life, is to not get too high with the highs and not get too low with the lows. It will take years of experience to reach that point. Talking about it is easy; doing it, is an entirely different matter. The author has worked on dozens of these cases and he still struggles with the emotional component. I am not sure that I will ever be able to follow my own advice, but if you are a young investigator or as we like to say a "true believer" you had better learn how to manage your emotions early in your career or you won't have a long one.

We have watched brilliant investigators, attorneys, professors and the like; literally sacrifice their physical health in the pursuit of justice for the wrongfully convicted. Heart attacks, strokes, emotional meltdowns are common. Divorces are as frequent as wind direction change. Financial ruin, commonplace as the change of seasons. The landscape is littered with the corpses of true believers. Beware, and be mindful of these pitfalls, they are around every corner.

Throughout this manuscript I have reiterated the importance of taking on cases that involve sentences that are less then death. To be sure a man or woman who receives the death penalty is in dire need of your services. Individuals who receive sentences of twenty, fifty, seventy five years and so forth are for all practical purposes serving a death sentence. The only significant difference is that individual is being slowly murdered. As a result I feel that they are every bit as needy as the individual sitting on death row.

The state has shifted gears and tactics. We have witnessed a strategy where on their own motion, they bring back an individual(s) for resentencing, remove the death penalty on a technicality and have the individual resentenced to life, or say 150 years. This is a slick little legal maneuver that takes away the stigma of the ultimate sentence and replaces it with something that will not nearly receive the public and media attention of which it was once worthy.

This clearly works on a number of levels. First and foremost as we in this criminal defense business realize, death penalty benefits magically disappear. In other words, the inmate who was on death row is now not eligible for a fraction of the financial aid that he was receiving because of his death row status. He or she has now been reduced to just another inmate with a long sentence.

The publicity, the appellate lawyers and state-funded investigators; mitigation specialist, etc., now all magically disappear. As far as the state is concerned, their job just got a whole lot easier. In fact, with few exceptions they have just gotten everything they always wanted. Neat, clean and quick, case closed, problem solved. How convenient is that?

So, in looking at the benefits of participating in a wrongful conviction case and weighing the negatives you may think that from our perspective we would recommend that you stay home. Work that fraud or insurance case. Don't dirty your hands with this bloody mess. Be safe, remain popular with law enforcement. Nonsense. We enjoy living out here on the edge

Is there a cause that is more important than an individual's freedom? Is there anything more precious then the ability to walk down the street a free man? We don't think so, and we are hopeful that if you have gotten this far, you agree with our basic premise that freedom is an individual's most important basic human right.

When Federal Judge Young imposed multiple life sentences on convicted shoe bomber terrorist Richard C. Reid on January 30, 2003, he stated in part at sentencing:

*"Here in this society, the very words carry freedom. They carry it everywhere from sea to shining sea. It is because we prize individual freedom so much that you are here in this beautiful courtroom. So that everyone can see, truly see that justice is administered fairly, individually and discretely." "It is for freedoms sake that your lawyers are striving so vigorously on your behalf and have filed appeals, will go in their representation of you before other judges. We are about it. Because we all know that the way we treat you, Mr. Reid is the measure of our own liberties. Make no mistake though. It is yet true that we will bear any burden, pay any price, to preserve our freedoms."*

Judge Young may have just described in that sentencing why we do what we do. We're not sure that Judge Young would agree with us, but we are hopeful that he was talking about the same thing that we are all striving for when we become involved in a wrongful conviction case.

Working in this business of criminal defense and eventually (quite by accident) wrongful conviction cases, has provided us with many hours of comic relief. (Otherwise we could not do this forever.) We're not sure at this point that we do this for the above-stated high ideals and the lofty echelons of truth and justice. We mean at the end of the day are we morally superior to our foes across the courtroom? Are we freeing bad guys and women so that they can become even bigger bad guys? The recidivism rate for the wrongfully convicted and freed is very high. Are we ultimately responsible for future bad acts? We hope not. In the end we can only concern ourselves with the case at hand.

Why do we jump with joy or look on with amazement when a prosecutor or law enforcement agency act on their own accord and voluntarily reexamine a wrongful conviction case? Is this such a rare occurrence in these matters that we are ready to hold a parade in their honor? We think that maybe, it is a rare and unusual occurrence. That is why there is such a need for a book such as this.

There is also a need for us in the private sector to recognize just what kind of talent pool lies within the public and appellate defender offices of the United States. To be certain, many of the wrongful conviction cases that we encounter are generated by the often inexcusable behavior and or performance of a singular public defenders office. They are an easy target for our clients and us. They are under-staffed, under funded, outspent and generally outmanned. The fault doesn't lie with the P.D.'s office. It is almost always a matter of funding. The fault lies with the legislative branch of the state legislature or congress.

We would dare say that with mature reflection, we have come to the conclusion that if our brethren in the public defender offices were as well funded as their counterparts in the prosecutor's office, this whole wrongful conviction crisis would become a minor problem. We will not see that in our lifetime so, it is really a fantasy at this place in time. Unless pressure is brought down upon the legislature to adequately fund the P.D.'s we will always have this reoccurring nightmare.

Writing this chapter was a pleasure. It has helped remind me why I do this for a living. If you have gotten the impression at any point that I was bragging or blowing my own horn, please forgive me. My motivation for writing this is my desire to see the wrongfully convicted set free. That's it.

As part of that pleasurable experience I get to recognize some of the heroes in the wrongful conviction arena. We would be remiss if we did not acknowledge former Illinois Governor George Ryan, Deputy Governor Matthew Betenhausen and the governor's press Secretary Dennis Culloton. In January 2003 just prior to Governor Ryan's term expiring we got to know the Governor and the aforemen-tioned individuals quite well. Knowing very well that they would be committing political suicide by their actions, they still had the courage to step up and do the right thing. Although Governor Ryan will go down in history as the hero or goat (depending on who's doing the writing) Betenhausen and Culloton's part in this was huge. They truly were warriors when they had to be.

Being present at DePaul University and Northwestern University in Chicago when Governor Ryan pardoned a number of our clients on death row and com-muted another 167 was one of those moments in time that made all the blood sweat and tears that we have shed throughout the years worthwhile. It is at moments like these that all of the grief, frustration and pain that one endures in this business become bearable.

This happened on January 10th & 11th of 2003. The road leading up to that day was to say the least, bumpy. Grand jury subpoenas, threats and intimidation from prosecutors and police alike were all the price of doing business. Participating and being at the center of the storm with our colleagues was a life altering experience. It was one of those moments that crystallize the reason for our struggle.

In Illinois and specifically the Chicago area, I am honored and blessed to work with a professional community of investigators, college professors, attorneys, innocence project coordinators, public defenders and other activists who never failed to fight the good fight. Their professional expertise and especially their character and heart always sustained us during the low moments. Like all families we have a squabble occasionally. But we always managed to put aside our differences for the good of the client.

Rob Warden and David Protess deserve special mention. They literally were the wrongful conviction movement in Chicago for many years. Long before anything called an "Innocence Project" came along Warden & Protess were in the trenches slugging it out with the authorities. Although neither one of them is an attorney, had no special interest in any of the victims we deal with, they were there alone and without resources before anyone else was. Between the two of them, nobody has done more or been more successful then they have in correcting these horrible wrongs.

The media in the Chicago area also deserves a special mention. Their willingness to take on "the system" is second to none. In the Chicago market there is an extraordinary pool of media talent that is as passionate about truth and justice as our other professional colleagues. There is little question that their reporting greatly influenced Governor Ryan in his historic mass commutations. They have and continue to "stir the drink."

At the end of the day we are in the business of saving the lives of innocent people. Is there a more noble undertaking then restoring an innocent person's freedom? We don't think so. This country was founded on the principals of freedom and the pursuit of happiness. It is extremely difficult to pursue these rights when one is locked away in a cage. Wrongful convictions happen for a variety of reasons.

Most Americans have the attitude that as long as it's not happening to me, "what do I care?" Do you recall the famous quote from WWII, "*When they came for the Jews, I didn't cry out because I wasn't a Jew. When they came for the Pole's I didn't cry out, because I wasn't a Pole. When they came for me, there was no one left to say anything"*. Fortunately for our clients there is a group of people out there who care and they care passionately.

If you are reading this book, you care. You are in that small but vocal and active minority that put it on the line everyday. You are doing God's work and you are saving innocent lives.

For that reason alone we salute you. Because without you and your efforts on behalf of the wrongfully convicted thousands of lives would have been lost. When you are feeling very alone, depressed and miserable think about what you are trying to accomplish. Think about Kenny Adams and his struggle and always remember that you are not alone in this fight for survival.

# 12

## *Internet Resource Chapter*

*Seek not, my soul, the life of the immortals;*
*But enjoy to the full the resources*
*That be within thy reach.*

*—Pindar*
*C 518-c 438 B.C.*
*Pythian Odes, IIS, 1.109*

The following are internet reference sites that the author has found useful. Because, the internet is constantly changing some sites may no longer exist or are out of date. I have attempted to keep this section as up to date as possible. Most of the web addresses are self explanatory.

### *Death Penalty Sites/Issues*

http://www.ojp.usdoj.gov/bjs/abstract/cp03.htm
**(Death Row Stats)**
http://www.abanet.org/deathpenalty
**(ABA Death Penalty Site)**
http://www.californiamoratorium.org/
http://www.deathpenalty.org/
http://www.mvfr.org/index.jsp
http://www.aclu.org/DeathPenalty/DeathPenaltyMain.cfm
http://www.amnestyusa.org/abolish/index.do
http://www.ncadp.org/
http://www.ccadp.org/

(Canadian Death Penalty Group)
http://www.nodeathpenalty.org/
http://www.worldcoalition.org/

*Freedom of Information Act Sites*

http://foia.state.gov/foia.htm
http://archive.aclu.org/library/foia.html
http://www.foia.com/
http://www.usdoj.gov/foia/other_age.htm

*Science & Lab Related Sites*
www.law-forensic.com
www.forensic-evidence.com
http://forensic.to/
www.forensicpage.com
www.corpus-delicti.com
www.kruglaw.com
www.forensic.to/forensic.html
www.forensicdna.com/
www.scientific.org/
www.ascid.org
www.aafs.com
www.theiai.org
www.criminalistics.com
www.afte.org
www.nafi.org
www.profiling.com
www.abfo.com
www.abft.com
www.polygraph.com
www.iabpa.com
http://www.csuchico.edu/anth/ABFA/

http://www.crime-scene-investigator.net/
http://www.xs4all.nl/~dacty/
http://www.crime-scene-investigator.net/


## *Law & Government*

http://news.findlaw.com/legalnews/lit/
http://www.publicrecordfinder.com/sexoffenders.html
(State sex offender sites)
http://news.surfwax.com/law/
http://bjsdata.ojp.usdoj.gov/dataonline/Search/Prosecutors/index.cfm
(Dept. Of Justice Prosecutor by County Stats)


## *Media Resources*
www.ire.org
http://www.justicedenied.org/
http://www.deathpenaltyinfo.org/article.php?did=412&scid=6
http://www.911-justice-phadp.org/
http://www.mediafinder.com/
(Media resources continued)


http://www.cyberjournalist.net/supersearch.php/
http://www.ibiblio.org/slanews/internet/archives.html
http://www.npr.org/
http://www.bizjournals.com/
http://www.loc.gov/rr/news/lists.html
http://www.cnn.com/
http://www.drudgereport.com/
http://www.suntimes.com/index/
http://mortgages.interest.com/content/general/top100.asp
(The Top 100 Newspapers)
http://www.ire.org/
http://store.publicintegrity.org/default.aspx

**(Prosecutorial Misconduct Data Base)**
http://www.law.com/index.shtml
http://www.rcfp.org/


*Innocence Projects*


http://www.innocenceproject.org/about/index.php
http://deathpenaltyinfo.org/
http://www.criminaljustice.org/
http://www.criminaljustice.org/
http://www.scu.edu/law/socialjustice/ncip_home.html
http://www.newenglandinnocence.org/
http://wcl.american.edu/innocenceproject/
http://www.nsulaw.nova.edu/fip/index.cfm
http://ga-innocenceproject.org/
http://www.law.northwestern.edu/wrongfulconvictions/
http://www.indylaw.indiana.edu/
http://www.uky.edu/Law/
http://www.ip-no.org/
http://wcl.american.edu/innocenceproject/
http://www.cooleylaw.edu/innocence/home.htm
http://www.ipmn.org/
http://www.rmicorg.com/
http://www.centurionministries.org
http://www.law.duke.edu/innocencecenter/
http://www.state.ok.us/~oids/
http://www.law.uh.edu/faculty/ddow2/dpage2/innocence.html
http://www.law.washington.edu/ipnw/
http://www.law.wisc.edu/FJR/innocence/index.htm
http://www.law.washington.edu/
http://www.neurolaw.com/Index.cfm?file=sources.htm

*Free Public Record Searches*

http://www.searchsystems.net/
http://www.lib.umich.edu/govdocs/
(University of Michigan Site Govt. Records)


*Knife Expert & State laws Governing Knives*

Bernard Levine's Knife Expert Witness Internet BizCard:
www.knife-expert.com


*Intellectual Property Digital Library, Patents, Trademarks*

http://www.wipo.int/ipdl/en/index.jsp
http://www.uspto.gov/patft/index.html
(Patents & Trademarks)


*Maps*

http://geography.about.com/library/maps/blindex.htm
http://www.mapquest.com/
http://plasma.nationalgeographic.com/mapmachine/
http://www.mapsonus.com/
http://www.alk.com/products/consumer/index.asp
http://www.lib.utexas.edu/maps/index.html


*Informant & Rat Site's*

http://whosarat.com/index.php
http://www.pbs.org/wgbh/pages/frontline/shows/snitch/

*Telephone Information*

http://www.tcpalaw.com/free/addr.htm
(Subpoena Contact Information from Carrier's)
http://www.tollfreephone.com/
(Toll Free Number Look Up)
http://www.aim-corp.com/swbull/wwareacode.htm#us
(Area Code Look up)
http://www.bigfoot.com/
http://fonefinder.net/


*Other Websites of Interest*

http://www.briefserve.com/home.asp
(Supreme Court Research Briefs)

http://lopucki.law.ucla.edu/contents_of_the_webbrd.htm
(Large Corporate Bankruptcies)

http://www.hipprogram.org/
(Horse Thief Information)

http://www.call21st.com/
(Forensic Animation Experts)

http://www.snopes.com/
(Urban legends)

http://www.blogcatalog.com/
(Everything You Ever Wanted to Know About BLOGS)

http://www.melissadata.com/ncoa/ncoa.htm
(Postal Information)

http://postinfo.net/html/
(More Postal Information)

http://www.find.com/(xc14rn55eagdy455q3eoey3q)/matchpoint.aspx
(Business Search Engine)

http://safedrivinginstitute.com/insurance.html
(Safe Driving Institute)

http://www.answers.com/


*Weather Information*

http://cirrus.sprl.umich.edu/wxnet/

http://www.nws.noaa.gov/

http://www.wunderground.com/

http://www.weather.com/?

http://www.washingtonpost.com/wp-srv/weather/historical/
historical.htm

http://www.pastweather.com/

*Personal*

Most of the people that you want to reach have websites listed above. However, if you need to reach either Attorney Craig Cooley or Fred Whitehurst (the Science gurus) please see below;

Craig Cooley
Craig_Cooley@fd.org
Federal Public Defender
Capitol Habeas Unit
333 South Third Street,
Suite 500, Las Vegas, Nevada
Phone: 702.388.6577

Fred Whitehurst
cfwhiteh@aol.com
Attorney at Law
P.O. Box 120
Bethel, NC, 27812
Phone: 252.825.1123

# *Governor George Ryan's Commutation Speech*

Below is the verbatim text of Governor Ryan's commutation speech given at Northwestern Law School in Chicago on January 10 2003. It was perhaps the most electric and historic moment in the history of the Death Penalty in the United States. It was certainly one of the most gratifying days in my long career. Sitting there front and center was an out of body experience. It is worth revisiting here.

"Four years ago I was sworn in as the 39th Governor of Illinois. That was just four short years ago; that's when I was a firm believer in the American System of Justice and the death penalty. I believed that the ultimate penalty for the taking of a life was administrated in a just and fair manner.

Today, 3 days before I end my term as Governor, I stand before you to explain my frustrations and deep concerns about both the administration and the penalty of death. It is fitting that we are gathered here today at Northwestern University with the students, teachers, lawyers and investigators who first shed light on the sorrowful condition of Illinois' death penalty system.

Professors Larry Marshall, Dave Protess have and their students along with investigators Paul Ciolino have gone above the call. They freed the falsely accused Ford Heights Four, they saved Anthony Porter's life, they fought for Rolando Cruz and Alex Hernandez. They devoted time and effort on behalf of Aaron Patterson, a young man who lost 15 years of his youth sitting among the condemned, and LeRoy Orange, who lost 17 of the best years of his life on death row.

It is also proper that we are together with dedicated people like Andrea Lyon who has labored on the front lines trying capital cases for many years and who is now devoting her passion to creating an innocence center at De Paul University. You saved Madison Hobley's life.

Together you spared the lives and secured the freedom of 17 men, men who were wrongfully convicted and rotting in the condemned units of our state prisons. What you have achieved is of the highest calling. Thank You!

Yes, it is right that I am here with you, where, in a manner of speaking, my journey from staunch supporters of capital punishment to reformer all began. But I must tell you, since the beginning of our journey, my thoughts and feelings about the death penalty have changed many, many times. I realize that over the course of my reviews I had said that I would not do blanket commutation. I have also said it was an option that was there and I would consider all options.

During my time in public office I have always reserved my right to change my mind if I believed it to be in the best public interest, whether it be about taxes, abortions or the death penalty. But I must confess that the debate with myself has been the toughest concerning the death penalty.

I suppose the reason the death penalty has been the toughest is because it is so final, the only public policy that determines who lives and who dies. In addition it is the only issue that attracts most of the legal minds across the country. I have received more advice on this issue than any other policy issue I have dealt with in my 35 years of public service. I have kept an open mind on both sides of the issues of commutation for life or death.

I have read, listened to and discussed the issue with the families of the victims as well as the families of the condemned. I know that any decision I make will not be accepted by one side or the other. I know that my decision will be just that—my decision, based on all the facts I could gather over the past 3 years. I may never be comfortable with my final decision, but I will know in my heart, that I did my very best to do the right thing. Having said that I want to share a story with you:

I grew up in Kankakee which even today is still a small midwestern town, a place where people tend to know each other. Steve Small was a neighbor. I watched him grow up. He would babysit my young children, which was not for the faint of heart since Lura Lynn and I had six children, 5 of them under the age of 3. He was a bright young man who helped run the family business. He got married and he and his wife had three children of their own. Lura

Lynn was especially close to him and his family. We took comfort in knowing he was there for us and we for him.

One September midnight he received a call at his home. There had been a break-in at the nearby house he was renovating. But as he left his house, he was seized at gunpoint by kidnappers. His captors buried him alive in a shallow hole. He suffocated to death before police could find him.

His killer led investigators to where Steve's body was buried. The killer, Danny Edward was also from my hometown. He now sits on death row. I also know his family. I share this story with you so that you know I do not come to this as a neophyte without having experienced a small bit of the bitter pill the survivors of murder must swallow.

My responsibilities and obligations are more than my neighbors and my family. I represent all the people of Illinois, like it or not. The decision I make about our criminal justice system is felt not only here but the world over.

The other day, I received a call from former South African President Nelson Mandela who reminded me that the United States sets the example for justice and fairness for the rest of the world. Today the United States is not in league with most of our major allies: Europe, Canada, Mexico, most of South and Central America. These countries rejected the death penalty. We are partners in death with several third world countries. Even Russia has called a moratorium.

The death penalty has been abolished in 12 states. In none of these states has the homicide rate increased. In Illinois last year we had about 1000 murders, only 2 percent of that 1000 were sentenced to death. Where is the fairness and equality in that? The death penalty in Illinois is not imposed fairly or uniformly because of the absence of standards for the 102 Illinois State Attorneys, who must decide whether to request the death sentence. Should geography be a factor in determining who gets the death sentence? I don't think so but in Illinois it makes a difference.

You are 5 times more likely to get a death sentence for first degree murder in the rural area of Illinois than you are in Cook County. Where is the justice and fairness in that? Where is the proportionality? Te Most Reverend Desmond Tutu wrote to me this week stating that "to take a life when a life has been lost is revenge, it is not justice. He says justice allows for mercy, clemency and compassion. These virtues are not weakness."

"In fact the most glaring weakness is that no matter how efficient and fair the death penalty may seem in theory, in actual practice it is primarily inflicted upon the weak, the poor, the ignorant and against racial minorities." That was a quote from Former California Governor Pat Brown. He wrote that in his book "Public Justice, Private Mercy" he wrote that nearly 50 years ago, nothing has changed in nearly 50 years.

I never intended to be an activist on this issue. I watched in surprise as freed death row inmate Anthony Porter was released from jail. A free man, he ran into the arms of Northwestern University Professor Dave Protess who poured his heart and soul into proving Porter's innocence with his journalism students.

He was 48 hours away from being wheeled into the execution chamber where the state would kill him.

It would all be so antiseptic and most of us would not have even paused, except that Anthony Porter was innocent of the double murder for which he had been condemned to die.After Mr. Porter's case there was the report by Chicago Tribune reporters Steve Mills and Ken Armstrong documenting the systemic failures of our capital punishment system. Half of the nearly 300 capital cases in Illinois had been reversed for a new trial or resentencing.Nearly Half!

33 of the death row inmates were represented at trial by an attorney who had later been disbarred or at some point suspended from practicing law.

Of the more than 160 death row inmates, 35 were African American defendants who had been convicted or condemned to die by all-white juries.
More than two-thirds of the inmates on death row were African American.
46 inmates were convicted on the basis of testimony from jailhouse informants.

I can recall looking at these cases and the information from the Mills/Armstrong series and asking my staff: How does that happen? How in God's name does that happen? I'm not a lawyer, so somebody explain it to me.
But no one could. Not to this day.

Then over the next few months. There were three more exonerated men, freed because their sentence hinged on a jailhouse informant or new DNA technology proved beyond a shadow of doubt their innocence. We then had the dubious distinction of exonerating more men than we had executed. 13 men found innocent, 12 executed.

As I reported yesterday, there is not a doubt in my mind that the number of innocent men freed from our Death Row stands at 17, with the pardons of Aaron Patterson, Madison Hobley, Stanley Howard and Leroy Orange.

That is an absolute embarrassment. 17 exonerated death row inmates is nothing short of a catastrophic failure. But the 13, now 17 men, is just the beginning of our sad arithmetic in prosecuting murder cases. During the time we have had capital punishment in Illinois, there were at least 33 other people wrongly convicted on murder charges and exonerated. Since we reinstated the death penalty there are also 93 people, 93, where our criminal justice system imposed the most severe sanction and later rescinded the sentence or even released them from custody because they were innocent.

How many more cases of wrongful conviction have to occur before we can all agree that the system is broken?

Throughout this process, I have heard many different points of view expressed. I have had the opportunity to review all of the cases involving the inmates on death row. I have conducted private group meetings, one in Springfield and one in Chicago, with the surviving family members of homicide victims. Everyone in the room who wanted to speak had the opportunity to do so. Some wanted to express their grief, others wanted to express their anger. I took it all in.

My commission and my staff had been reviewing each and every case for three years. But, I redoubled my effort to review each case personally in order to respond to the concerns of prosecutors and victims' families. This individual review also naturally resulted in a collective examination of our entire death penalty system.

I also had a meeting with a group of people who are less often heard from, and who are not as popular with the media. The family members of death row inmates have a special challenge to face. I spent an afternoon with those family members at a Catholic Church here in Chicago. At that meeting, I heard a different kind of pain expressed. Many of these families live with the twin pain of knowing not only that, in some cases, their family member may have been responsible for inflicting a terrible trauma on another family, but also the pain of knowing that society has called for another killing. These parents, siblings and children are not to blame for the crime committed, yet these innocent stand to have their loved ones killed by the state. As Mr. Mandela told me, they are also branded and scarred for life because of the awful crime committed by their family member.

Others were even more tormented by the fact that their loved one was another victim, that they were truly innocent of the crime for which they were sentenced to die.

It was at this meeting that I looked into the face of Claude Lee, the father of Eric Lee, who was convicted of killing Kankakee police officer Anthony Samfay a few years ago. It was a traumatic moment, once again, for my hometown. A brave officer, part of that thin blue line that protects each of us, was struck down by wanton violence. If you will kill a police officer, you have absolutely no respect for the laws of man or God.

I've know the Lee family for a number of years. There does not appear to be much question that Eric was guilty of killing the officer. However, I can say now after our review, there is also not much question that Eric is seriously ill, with a history of treatment for mental illness going back a number of years.

The crime he committed was a terrible one, killing a police officer. Society demands that the highest penalty be paid. But I had to ask myself: could I send another man's son to death under the deeply flawed system of capital punishment we have in Illinois? A troubled young man, with a history of mental illness? Could I rely on the system of justice we have in Illinois not to make another horrible mistake? Could I rely on a fair sentencing?

In the United States the overwhelming majority of those executed are psychotic, alcoholic, drug addicted or mentally unstable. The frequently are raised in an impoverished and abusive environment.

Seldom are people with money or prestige convicted of capital offenses, even more seldom are they executed. To quote Governor Brown again, he said "society has both the right and the moral duty to protect itself against its enemies. This natural and prehistoric axiom has never successfully been refuted. If by ordered death, society is really protected and our homes and institutions guarded, then even the most extreme of all penalties can be justified."

"Beyond its honor and incredibility, it has neither protected the innocent nor deterred the killers. Publicly sanctioned killing has cheapened human life and dignity without the redeeming grace which comes from justice metered out swiftly, evenly, humanely." At stake throughout the clemency process, was whether some, all or none of these inmates on death row would have their sentences commuted from death to life without the possibility parole.

One of the things discussed with family members was life without parole was seen as a life filled with perks and benefits. Some inmates on death row don't want a sentence of life without parole. Danny Edwards wrote me and told me not to do him any favors because he didn't want to face a prospect of a life in prison without parole. They will be confined in a cell that is about 5-feet-by-12 feet, usually double-bunked. Our prisons have no air conditioning, except at our supermax facility where inmates are kept in their cell 23 hours a day. In summer months, temperatures in these prisons exceed one hundred degrees. It is a stark and dreary existence. They can think about their crimes. Life without parole has even, at times, been described by prosecutors as a fate worse than death.

Yesterday, I mentioned a lawsuit in Livingston County where a judge ruled the state corrections department cannot force feed two corrections inmates who are on a hunger strike. The judge ruled that suicide by hunger strike was not an irrational action by the inmates, given what their future holds.

Earlier this year, the U.S. Supreme Court held that it is unconstitutional and cruel and unusual punishment to execute the mentally retarded. It is now the law of the land. How many people have we already executed who were mentally retarded and are now dead and buried? Although we now know that they have been killed by the state unconstitutionally and illegally. Is that fair? Is that right?

This court decision was last spring. The General Assembly failed to pass any measure defining what constitutes mental retardation. We are a rudderless ship because they failed to act. This is even after the Illinois Supreme Court also told lawmakers that it is their job and it must be done.

I started with this issue concerned about innocence. But once I studied, once I pondered what had become of our justice system, I came to care above all about fairness. Fairness is fundamental to the American system of justice and our way of life. The facts I have seen in reviewing each and every one of these cases raised questions not only about the innocence of people on death row, but about the fairness of the death penalty system as a whole.

If the system was making so many errors in determining whether someone was guilty in the first place, how fairly and accurately was it determining which guilty defendants deserved to live and which deserved to die? What effect was race having? What effect was poverty having? And in almost every one of the exonerated 17, we not only have breakdowns in the system with police, prosecutors and judges, we have terrible cases of shabby defense lawyers.

There is just no way to sugar coat it. There are defense attorneys that did not consult with their clients, did not investigate the case and were completely unqualified to handle complex death penalty cases. They often didn't put much effort into fighting a death sentence. If your life is on the line, your lawyer ought to be fighting for you. As I have said before, there is more than enough blame to go around.

I had more questions. In Illinois, I have learned, we have 102 decision makers. Each of them are politically elected, each beholden to the demands of their community and, in some cases, to the media or especially vocal victims' families. In cases that have the attention of the media and the public, are decisions

to seek the death penalty more likely to occur? What standards are these prosecutors using?

Some people have assailed my power to commute sentences, a power that literally hundreds of legal scholars from across the country have defended. But
prosecutors in Illinois have the ultimate commutation power, a power that is
exercised every day. They decide who will be subject to the death penalty, who
will get a plea deal or even who may get a complete pass on prosecution. By
what objective standards do they make these decisions? We do not know, they
are not public.

There were more than 1000 murders last year in Illinois. There is no doubt
that all murders are horrific and cruel. Yet, less than 2 percent of those murder
defendants will receive the death penalty. That means more than 98% of victims families do not get, and will not receive whatever satisfaction can be
derived from the execution of the murderer.

Moreever, if you look at the cases, as I have done, both individually and collectively—a killing with the same circumstances might get 40 years in one
county and death in another county. I have also seen where co-defendants
who are equally or even more culpable get sentenced to a term of years, while
another less culpable defendant ends up on death row.

In my case-by-case review, I found three people that fell into this category,
Mario Flores, Montel Johnson and William Franklin. Today I have com-
muted their sentences to a term of 40 years to bring their sentences into line
with their co-defendants and to reflect the other extraordinary circumstances
of these cases.

Supreme Court Justice Potter Stewart has said that the imposition of the
death penalty on defendants in this country is as freakish and arbitrary as who
gets hit by a bolt of lightning.

For years the criminal justice system defended and upheld the imposition of
the death penalty for the 17 exonerated inmates from Illinois Death row. Yet
when the real killers are charged, prosecutors have often sought sentences of
less than death. In the Ford Heights Four Case, Verneal Jimerson and Dennis
Williams fought the death sentences imposed upon them for 18 years before
they were exonerated. Later, Cook County prosecutors sought life in prison
for two of the real killers and a sentence of 80 years for a third.

What made the murder for which the Ford Heights Four were sentenced to
die less heinous and worthy of the death penalty twenty years later with a new
set of defendants?

We have come very close to having our state Supreme Court rule our death penalty statute—the one that I helped enact in 1977—unconstitutional. Former State Supreme Court Justice Seymour Simon wrote to me that it was only happenstance that our statute was not struck down by the state's high court. When he joined the bench in 1980, three other justices had already said Illinois' death penalty was unconstitutional. But they got cold feet when a case came along to revisit the question. One judge wrote that he wanted to wait and see if the Supreme Court of the United States would rule on the constitutionality of the new Illinois law. Another said precedent required him to follow the old state Supreme Court ruling with which he disagreed.

Even a pharmacist knows that doesn't make sense. We wouldn't have a death penalty today, and we all wouldn't be struggling with this issue, if those votes had been different. How rbitrary.

Several years after we enacted our death penalty statute, Girvies Davis was executed. Justice Simon writes that he was executed because of this unconstitutional aspect of the Illinois law—the wide latitude that each Illinois State's Attorney has to determine what cases qualify for the death penalty. One State's Attorney waived his request for the death sentence when Davis' first sentencing was sent back to the trial court for a new sentencing hearing. The prosecutor was going to seek a life sentence. But in the interim, a new State's Attorney took office and changed directions. He once again sought and secured a death sentence. Davies was executed.

How fair is that?After the flaws in our system were exposed, the Supreme Court of Illinois took it upon itself to begin to reform its' rules and improve the trial of capital cases. It changed the rule to require that State's Attorney's give advance notice to defendants that they plan to seek the death penalty to require notice before trial instead of after conviction. The Supreme Court also enacted new discovery rules designed to prevent trials by ambush and to allow for better investigation of cases from the beginning.

But shouldn't that mean if you were tried or sentenced before the rules changed, you ought to get a new trial or sentencing with the new safeguards of the rules? This issue has divided our Supreme Court, some saying yes, a majority saying no. These justices have a lifetime of experience with the criminal justice system and it concerns me that these great minds so strenuously differ on an issue of such importance, especially where life or death hangs in the balance.

What are we to make of the studies that showed that more than 50% of Illinois jurors could not understand the confusing and obscure sentencing instructions that were being used? What effect did that problem have on the trustworthiness of death sentences? A review of the cases shows that often even the lawyers and judges are confused about the instructions—let alone the jurors sitting in judgment. Cases still come before the Supreme Court with arguments about whether the jury instructions were proper.

I spent a good deal of time reviewing these death row cases. My staff, many of whom are lawyers, spent busy days and many sleepless nights answering my questions, providing me with information, giving me advice. It became clear to me that whatever decision I made, I would be criticized. It also became clear to me that it was impossible to make reliable choices about whether our capital punishment system had really done its job.

As I came closer to my decision, I knew that I was going to have to face the question of whether I believed so completely in the choice I wanted to make that I could face the prospect of even commuting the death sentence of Daniel Edwards, the man who had killed a close family friend of mine. I discussed it with my wife, Lura Lynn, who has stood by me all these years. She was angry and disappointed at my decision like many of the families of other victims will be.

I was struck by the anger of the families of murder victims. To a family they talked about closure. They pleaded with me to allow the state to kill an inmate in its name to provide the families with closure. But is that the purpose of capital punishment? Is it to soothe the families? And is that truly what the families experience.

I cannot imagine losing a family member to murder. Nor can I imagine spending every waking day for 20 years with a single minded focus to execute the killer. The system of death in Illinois is so unsure that it is not unusual for cases to take 20 years before they are resolved. And thank God. If it had moved any faster, then Anthony Porter, the Ford Heights Four, Ronald Jones, Madison Hobley and the other innocent men we've exonerated might be dead and buried.

But it is cruel and unusual punishment for family members to go through this pain, this legal limbo for 20 years. Perhaps it would be less cruel if we sentenced the killers to TAMS to life, and used our resources to better serve victims.

My heart ached when I heard one grandmother who lost children in an arson fire. She said she could not afford proper grave markers for her grandchildren who died. Why can't the state help families provide a proper burial?

Another crime victim came to our family meetings. He believes an inmate sent to death row for another crime also shot and paralyzed him. The inmate he says gets free health care while the victim is struggling to pay his substantial medical bills and, as a result, he has forgone getting proper medical care to alleviate the physical pain he endures.

What kind of victims services are we providing? Are all of our resources geared toward providing this notion of closure by execution instead of tending to the physical and social service needs of victim families? And what kind of values are we instilling in these wounded families and in the young people? As Gandhi said, an eye for an eye only leaves the whole world blind.

President Lincoln often talked of binding up wounds as he sought to preserve the Union. "We are not enemies, but friends. We must not be enemies. Though passion may have strained, it must not break our bonds of affection."

I have had to consider not only the horrible nature of the crimes that put men on death row in the first place, the terrible suffering of the surviving family members of the victims, the despair of the family members of the inmates, but I have also had to watch in frustration as members of the Illinois General Assembly failed to pass even one substantive death penalty reform. Not one. They couldn't even agree on ONE. How much more evidence is needed before the General Assembly will take its responsibility in this area seriously?

The fact is that the failure of the General Assembly to act is merely a symptom of the larger problem. Many people express the desire to have capital punishment. Few, however, seem prepared to address the tough questions that arise when the system fails. It is easier and more comfortable for politicians to be tough on crime and support the death penalty. It wins votes. But when it comes to admitting that we have a problem, most run for cover. Prosecutors across our state continue to deny that our death penalty system is broken, or they say if there is a problem, it is really a small one and we can fix it somehow. It is difficult to see how the system can be fixed when not a single one of the reforms proposed by my Capital Punishment Commission has been adopted. Even the reforms the prosecutors agree with haven't been adopted.

So when will the system be fixed? How much more risk can we afford? Will we actually have to execute an innocent person before the tragedy that is our capital punishment system in Illinois is really understood? This summer, a United States District court judge held the federal death penalty was unconstitutional and noted that with the number of recent exonerations based on DNA and new scientific technology we undoubtedly executed innocent people before this technology emerged.

As I prepare to leave office, I had to ask myself whether I could really live with the prospect of knowing that I had the opportunity to act, but that I failed to do so because I might be criticized. Could I take the chance that our capital punishment system might be reformed, that wrongful convictions might not occur, that enterprising journalism students might free more men from death row? A system that's so fragile that it depends on young journalism students is seriously flawed.

"There is no honorable way to kill, no gentle way to destroy. There is nothing good in war. Except its ending." That's what Abraham Lincoln said about the bloody war between the states. It was a war fought to end the sorriest chapter in American history—the institution of slavery. While we are not in a civil war now, we are facing what is shaping up to be one of the great civil rights struggles of our time. Stephen Bright of the Southern Center for Human Rights has taken the position that the death penalty is being sought with increasing frequency in some states against the poor and minorities.

Our own study showed that juries were more likely to sentence to death if the victim were white than if the victim were black—three-and-a-half times more likely to be exact. We are not alone. Just this month Maryland released a study of their death penalty system and racial disparities exist there too.

This week, Mamie Till died. Her son Emmett was lynched in Mississippi in the 1950s. She was a strong advocate for civil rights and reconciliation. In fact just three weeks ago, she was the keynote speaker at the Murder Victims' Families for Reconciliation Event in Chicago. This group, many of whom I've met, opposes the death penalty even though their family members have been lost to senseless killing. Mamie's strength and grace not only ignited the civil rights movement—including inspiring Rosa Parks to refuse to go to the back of the bus—but inspired murder victims' families until her dying day.

Is our system fair to all? Is justice blind? These are important human rights issues. Another issue that came up in my individual, case-by-case review was the issue of international law. The Vienna Convention protects U.S. citizens abroad and foreign nationals in the United States. It provides that if you arrested, you should be afforded the opportunity to contact your consulate. There are five men on death row who were denied that internationally recognized human right. Mexico's President Vicente Fox contacted me to express his deep concern for the Vienna Convention violations. If we do not uphold international law here, we cannot expect our citizens to be protected outside the United States.

My Commission recommended the Supreme Court conduct a proportionality review of our system in Illinois. While our appellate courts perform a case by case review of the appellate record, they have not done such a big picture study. Instead, we tinker with a case-by-case review as each appeal lands on their docket.

In 1994, near the end of his distinguished career on the Supreme Court of the United States, Justice Harry Blackmun wrote an influential dissent in the body of law on capital punishment. 20 years earlier he was part of the court that issued the landmark Furman decision. The Court decided that the death penalty statutes in use throughout the country were fraught with severe flaws that rendered them unconstitutional. Quite frankly, they were the same problems we see here in Illinois. To many, it looked liked the Furman decision meant the end of the death penalty in the United States.

This was not the case. Many states responded to Furman by developing and enacting new and improved death penalty statutes. In 1976, four years after it had decided Furman, Justice Blackmun joined the majority of the United States Supreme Court in deciding to give the States a chance with these new and improved death penalty statutes. There was great optimism in the air.

This was the climate in 1977, when the Illinois legislature was faced with the momentous decision of whether to reinstate the death penalty in Illinois. I was a member of the General Assembly at that time and when I pushed the green button in favor of reinstating the death penalty in this great State, I did so with the belief that whatever problems had plagued the capital punishment system in the past were now being cured. I am sure that most of my colleagues who voted with me that day shared that view.

But 20 years later, after affirming hundreds of death penalty decisions, Justice Blackmun came to the realization, in the twilight of his distinguished career that the death penalty remains fraught with arbitrariness, discrimination, caprice and mistake." He expressed frustration with a 20-year struggle to develop procedural and substantive safeguards. In a now famous dissent he wrote in 1994, "From this day forward, I no longer shall tinker with the machinery of death."

One of the few disappointments of my legislative and executive career is that the General Assembly failed to work with me to reform our deeply flawed system.
I don't know why legislators could not heed the rising voices of reform. I don't know how many more systemic flaws we needed to uncover before they would be spurred to action.

Three times I proposed reforming the system with a package that would restrict the use of jailhouse snitches, create a statewide panel to determine death eligible cases, and reduce the number of crimes eligible for death. These reforms would not have created a perfect system, but they would have dramatically reduced the chance for error in the administration of the ultimate penalty.

The Governor has the constitutional role in our state of acting in the interest of justice and fairness. Our state constitution provides broad power to the Governor to issue reprieves, pardons and commutations. Our Supreme Court has reminded inmates petitioning them that the last resort for relief is the governor.

At times the executive clemency power has perhaps been a crutch for courts to avoid making the kind of major change that I believe our system needs.
Our systemic case-by-case review has found more cases of innocent men wrongfully sentenced to death row. Because our three year study has found only more questions about the fairness of the sentencing; because of the spectacular failure to reform the system; because we have seen justice delayed for countless death row inmates with potentially meritorious claims; because the Illinois death penalty system is arbitrary and capricious—and therefore immoral—I no longer shall tinker with the machinery of death. I cannot say it more eloquently than Justice Blackmun.

The legislature couldn't reform it.
Lawmakers won't repeal it.
But I will not stand for it.
I must act.

Our capital system is haunted by the demon of error, error in determining guilt, and error in determining who among the guilty deserves to die. Because of all of these reasons today I am commuting the sentences of all death row inmates.

This is a blanket commutation. I realize it will draw ridicule, scorn and anger from many who oppose this decision. They will say I am usurping the decisions of judges and juries and state legislators. But as I have said, the people of our state have vested in me to act in the interest of justice. Even if the exercise of my power becomes my burden I will bear it. Our constitution compels it. I sought this office, and even in my final days of holding it I cannot shrink from the obligations to justice and fairness that it demands.

There have been many nights where my staff and I have been deprived of sleep in order to conduct our exhaustive review of the system. But I can tell you this: I will sleep well knowing I made the right decision.

As I said when I declared the moratorium, it is time for a rational discussion on the death penalty. While our experience in Illinois has indeed sparked a debate, we have fallen short of a rational discussion. Yet if I did not take this action, I feared that there would be no comprehensive and thorough inquiry into the guilt of the individuals on death row or of the fairness of the sentences applied.

To say it plainly one more time—the Illinois capital punishment system is broken. It has taken innocent men to a hair's breadth escape from their unjust execution. Legislatures past have refused to fix it. Our new legislature and our

new Governor must act to rid our state of the shame of threatening the innocent with execution and the guilty with unfairness.

In the days ahead, I will pray that we can open our hearts and provide something
for victims' families other than the hope of revenge. Lincoln once said: "I have
always found that mercy bears richer fruits than strict justice." I can only hope
that will be so. God bless you. And God bless the people of Illinois."

# Postscript

*"But we were born of risen apes, not fallen angels, and the apes were armed killers besides. And so what shall we wonder at? Our murders and massacres and missiles, and our irreconcilable regiments? Or our treaties whatever they may be worth; our symphonies however seldom they may be played; our peaceful acres, however frequently they may be converted into battlefields; our dreams however rarely they may be accomplished. The miracle of man is not how far he has sunk but how magnificently he has risen. We are known among the stars by our poems, not our corpses."*

—*Robert Ardrey*

I have been around this criminal justice system for thirty years now. I like to think that I have learned a few things. Mature reflection will do that. I am indebted to the brilliant and brave people that have nurtured and taught me throughout the years. I have come full circle with respect to the death penalty. I have traveled far and I have been exposed to far too much injustice in life. If I have learned one lesson it is that the death penalty does not deter crime. It does not persuade one idiot from picking up a weapon and shooting one or fifteen people. However, it does make for great political rhetoric.

The death penalty is about politics. It is the proverbial line in the sand between conservatives and liberals. Outside of abortion there is not a more controversial subject in the United States. I have always wondered how one could be so against abortion and so for the death penalty. If there ever was a moral conflict in life, there it is.

Notwithstanding your view on this subject there is one final point. If you kill someone in the name of justice and they are innocent, how do we compensate that *victim's* family or loved ones? Do we put the prosecutor and police officers on trial for murder, convict them, and then murder them? Do we give a few million to the victim's family? I don't know what would be fair at that point. I do know that we aren't going to rectify the problem later, as that is a fairly final act.

This book is not meant to be the final and great authority on death penalty or wrongful convictions. It will hopefully motivate some of you. Some of the people reading this may find just one thing helpful, something they hadn't thought of in a while. I don't know what it would be. But, I do know that throughout my long career, it has been the little things that mattered. It was the bits and pieces that I picked up here and there that put certain investigations over the top. It was with that purpose that I wrote this book.

There is no one authority on this subject. I've met a few people who think they are the world authority, but it always comes down to a team effort. This is the secret to the successful conclusion in the wrongful conviction case.

# About The Author

Paul Ciolino is a lifelong resident of Chicago. He is a seven-year veteran of the United States Army and the co-founder and former chief of the Child Homicide Unit for the Illinois Department of Children & Family Services. He has been a private investigator since 1981.

He has been awarded dozens of commendations from both government and private industry including: The International Investigator of The Year Award, The Louisiana Investigator of The Year Award and The Dante Award, which is awarded for an individual's pursuit of justice. He is the only non-journalist to have been awarded that honor in its 38-year history. CBS News' Dan Rather has called Ciolino "One of America's five best investigators."

He has been instrumental in freeing five men from death row in Illinois and three more from life sentences in Illinois prisons. In 1999, Illinois Governor George Ryan issued the first-ever death penalty moratorium after Ciolino secured a videotaped confession in a 19-year-old double homicide *for which an innocent man had been convicted.* In 2003, when former Governor Ryan granted clemency and pardons to 167 Illinois death row inmates, he cited Paul Ciolino's work as one of his main reasons for doing so.

Ciolino is a past president and life member of The Special Agents Association. Past president of The National Association of Legal Investigators and two-term board member of The Council of International Investigators. He holds a number of professional designations, such as Certified Fraud Examiner, Certified International Investigator and Board Certified Forensic Examiner.

He is the co-author of several books: *Advanced Forensic Civil Investigations, Advanced Forensic Criminal Defense Investigations, Corporate Investigations*, published by Lawyers & Judges Publishing Company, Tucson, Ariz.; and *Investigation Manual,* published by The Center for Justice in Capital Cases, DePaul University College of Law, 2004.

He has been featured in dozens of magazine and news articles throughout the world. Television specials in the U.S., Canada, Japan, Germany, France and other western countries have highlighted his work in wrongful convictions. He is currently involved with Oscar & Emmy winner Abby Mann (*Judgment at Nuremberg, The McMartin Preschool Story*, and *Biography of Martin Luther King*) in developing a movie and television series on his life.

He can be reached through his website at: www.pjcinvestigations.com

978-0-595-34813-8
0-595-34813-0

Printed in the United States
134207LV00004B/5/A

9 780595 348138